"At last I caught what I was listening for—the long-drawn quavering howl from over the hills, a sound as wild and indigenous to the north as the muskegs or the northern lights. That was wilderness music, something as free and untamed as there is on this earth."
—Sigurd Olson, The Singing Wilderness *(1951)*

The Wolves of Minnesota
HOWL in the HEARTLAND

L. DAVID MECH, EDITOR

Voyageur Press

Editor: L. David Mech
Voyageur Press In-House Editor: Amy Rost-Holtz
Designer: Kjerstin Moody
Maps and graphs by: Maria Friedrich
Printed in Hong Kong

00 01 02 03 04 5 4 3 2 1

Library of Congress Cataloging-in-Publication Data available

ISBN 0-89658-464-X

Distributed in Canada by Raincoast Books, 9050 Shaughnessy Street, Vancouver, B.C. V6P 6E5

Published by Voyageur Press, Inc.
123 North Second Street, P.O. Box 338, Stillwater, MN 55082 U.S.A.
651-430-2210, fax 651-430-2211
books@voyageurpress.com
www.voyageurpress.com

Educators, fundraisers, premium and gift buyers, publicists, and marketing managers:
Looking for creative products and new sales ideas? Voyageur Press books are available at special discounts when purchased in quantities, and special editions can be created to your specifications. For details contact the marketing department at 800-888-9653.

Page 1: (Photograph © Michael H. Francis)
Pages 2–3: How should Minnesota manage its recovered wolf population? This question is at the heart of an intense ongoing debate because humans on all sides view wolves with strong emotion. (Photograph © D. Robert Franz)
Facing page: While mottled gray is the most common color of Minnesota's wolves, about 3 percent have jet black fur and a very few have creamy white coats. (Photograph © Michael H. Francis)

Dedication

This book is dedicated to Sigurd Olson, who not only conducted the first field study of the wolf in Minnesota and arguably in the world, but, more importantly, whose eloquent writings and courageous efforts helped preserve the Minnesota wilderness. This wilderness formed the refuge and reservoir that allowed wolves to survive in Minnesota when, except for those in Isle Royale National Park, they had been exterminated from the remainder of the contiguous United States.

Acknowledgments

During preparation of this book, I was employed by the Biological Resources Division of the U.S. Geological Survey. This division was formerly known as the National Biological Service, the National Biological Survey, and the Division of Wildlife Research of the U.S. Fish and Wildlife Service. Much of the research whose results are summarized and interpreted here for the public was completed and published while I was in the employ of these agencies.

Many other agencies and individuals also contributed to the research. The U.S. Department of Agriculture North Central Research Station (formerly North Central Forest Experiment Station) contributed financial and logistical support for the research. The Superior National Forest and the Special Projects Foundation assisted with financial support, and the Minnesota Department of Natural Resources granted permits and provided published and unpublished data. Numerous volunteer wildlife technicians assisted with much of the field work, and many pilots provided safe flying for data collection.

Finally, the following people critiqued an earlier draft of this book and offered many helpful suggestions for improving it: Steve Fritts, Nancy Gibson, Ron Kirby, Walter Medwid, Bill Paul, and Nancy Jo Tubbs.

I thank all of the above.

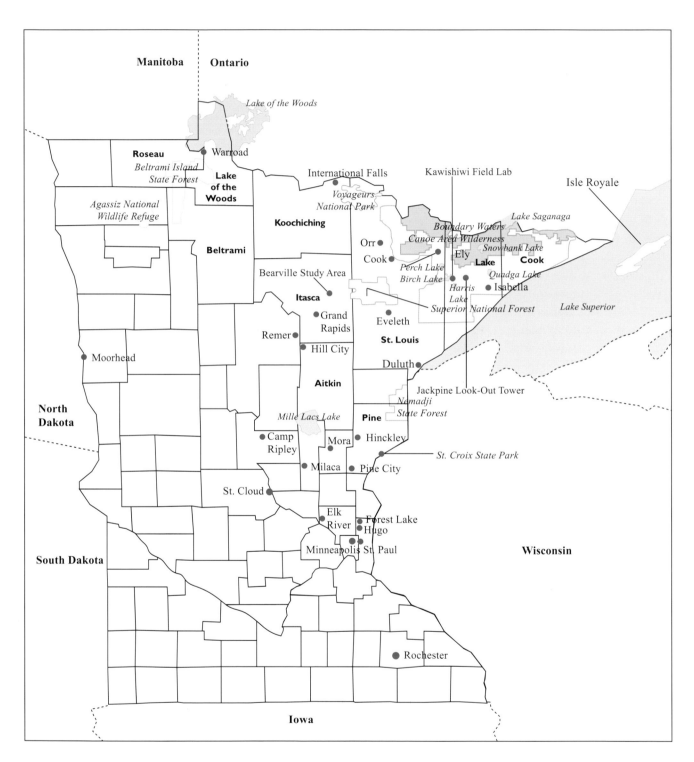

Manitoba   Ontario

Lake of the Woods

Roseau   ● Warroad

Beltrami Island
State Forest

Lake
of the
Woods

International Falls

Kawishiwi Field Lab

Isle Royale

Agassiz National
Wildlife Refuge

Voyageurs
National Park

Lake Saganaga

Koochiching

Boundary Waters
Canoe Area Wilderness

Beltrami

Orr ●

Snowbank Lake

●
Cook

Ely

Lake   **Cook**

Perch Lake

Quadga Lake

Bearville Study Area

Birch Lake

● Isabella

Itasca   ●

Harris
Lake

Lake Superior

● Grand
Rapids

Eveleth

Superior National Forest

Remer ●

● Eveleth

● Hill City

St. Louis

Moorhead ●

Aitkin

Duluth ●

North
Dakota

Jackpine Look-Out Tower

Mille Lacs Lake

Nemadji
State Forest

Pine

Camp ●
Ripley

● Mora

● Hinckley

St. Croix State Park

● Milaca

Pine City
●

South Dakota

St. Cloud ●

Elk ●
River

● Forest Lake
● Hugo

Wisconsin

Minneapolis ● St. Paul

● Rochester

Iowa

Cities, counties, lakes, and other areas mentioned throughout the book.

Contents

Introduction

by L. David Mech

Minnesota. The name of the state conjures up visions of pristine wilderness, sparkling lakes, tall pines, and howling wolves. And rightly so. Lying just south of the Canadian border, a large portion of Minnesota's wilderness—really a southern extension of the great Canadian boreal forest—has been preserved completely through the twentieth century. Along with it, the state has also saved the premiere denizen and symbol of forested wilderness, the wolf.

Minnesota is the only one of the forty-eight contiguous states that managed to harbor the wolf while all the others deliberately exterminated the species, primarily through extensive campaigns of poisoning and persistent persecution. (Technically, nearby Michigan also kept some wolves, a small population that in 1949 colonized Isle Royale National Park in Lake Superior. But Michigan's mainland wolves were about gone by the early 1970s.)

The Minnesota wolf population probably never dropped lower than about 650, primarily because of the Boundary Waters Canoe Area Wilderness (BWCAW), an area so inaccessible to humans except by foot or canoe that wolves were never wiped out of it or surrounding areas. Of course, like all of North America—all of the northern hemisphere for that matter—Minnesota once supported wolves throughout the state. Wolves eat mainly hoofed mammals such as moose, deer, elk, caribou, and bison, and Minnesota was home to all of these prey.

Unlike neighboring Wisconsin and Michigan, which are separated from Canada by magnificent Lake Superior, Minnesota is merely politically separated. And as numerous northern Minnesotans have intoned for decades, "The Canadian wolves don't pay any attention to the border."

Thus, as most of Minnesota killed off its wolves, they were constantly replenished by the dispersal of their Canadian relatives and those from Minnesota's million-acre wilderness. Not so for Wisconsin and Michigan. When these states exterminated their wolves (outside of Isle

Facing page: The wolf's elusive nature has helped make it a symbol of the wilderness and a rallying point for people who value the environment. (Photograph © D. Robert Franz)
Inset: Minnesota is the only one of the forty-eight contiguous states where the wolf was never exterminated. The limited accessibility to Minnesota's extensive wilderness helped to hinder the widespread poisoning that went on elsewhere in the country. (Photograph © Layne Kennedy)

Above: The wolf is one of the world's most studied animals. Considerable information is available about the nature of the wolf: its social life, the composition of the pack in which it lives, its movements, reproduction, survival, and mortality. (Photograph © Alan & Sandy Carey)

Overleaf: Entire wolf packs were wiped out by poison. In addition, den digging and pup destruction, as well as aerial hunting, helped eliminate whole packs. (Photograph © L. David Mech)

Royale) by the late 1960s, there was no extensive wilderness or ready route from the great Canadian reservoir. In these states, the public began to wonder "Will we ever hear the howl of the wolf again?"

The Endangered Species Act of 1973 totally protected the remnant wolf population in Minnesota and provided the basis for a complete reversal in the fate of the wolf in the Lake Superior states. It fostered basic research, legal protection, and public education, including the founding of the International Wolf Center.

In winter, 1997–98, the Minnesota wolf population stood at an estimated 2,450 animals, and was increasing by more than 100 wolves per year. While some think this number may be too high for the wolf's own good, others applaud the wolf's return to so many of its old haunts. Having also repopulated Wisconsin and Michigan, the animal is now on the verge of being removed from the federal government's endangered species list in all three states.

The Wolves of Minnesota, written by several of the people who have studied Minnesota wolves, features the fascinating story of the comeback of the wolf in Minnesota, including the animal's basic biology. It also examines the cultural costs of that recovery, as Minnesota's wolf managers, wolf enthusiasts, and general public are asking themselves not "Will we ever hear the howl of the wolf again?" but "How many howls are enough?" In short, the goal of this book is to present for the public the Minnesota wolf as science knows it, and to explore ecologically and socially sound ways of managing the animal.

Chapters 1, 2, and 3 provide background about the wolf in Minnesota, examining the animal and its packs and populations; the past, present, and future ranges of the species in Minnesota; and the rich history of scientific research about the animal.

Chapters 4 through 7 detail the biology of the Minnesota wolf, the nature and makeup of the pack, how packs fit into the population, what keeps packs apart, how the wolves reproduce and move about their range, how they perish, and how the lives of the wolf and its prey—the deer and moose—are so intertwined that features of each are readily explained by their interactions with the others.

Chapter 8 examines wolf-human interactions. Minnesota alone among the forty-eight contiguous states has lived continually with the wolf. What has been learned? How do Minnesotans feel about this controversial creature? And most importantly, what is the future of the wolf in Minnesota?

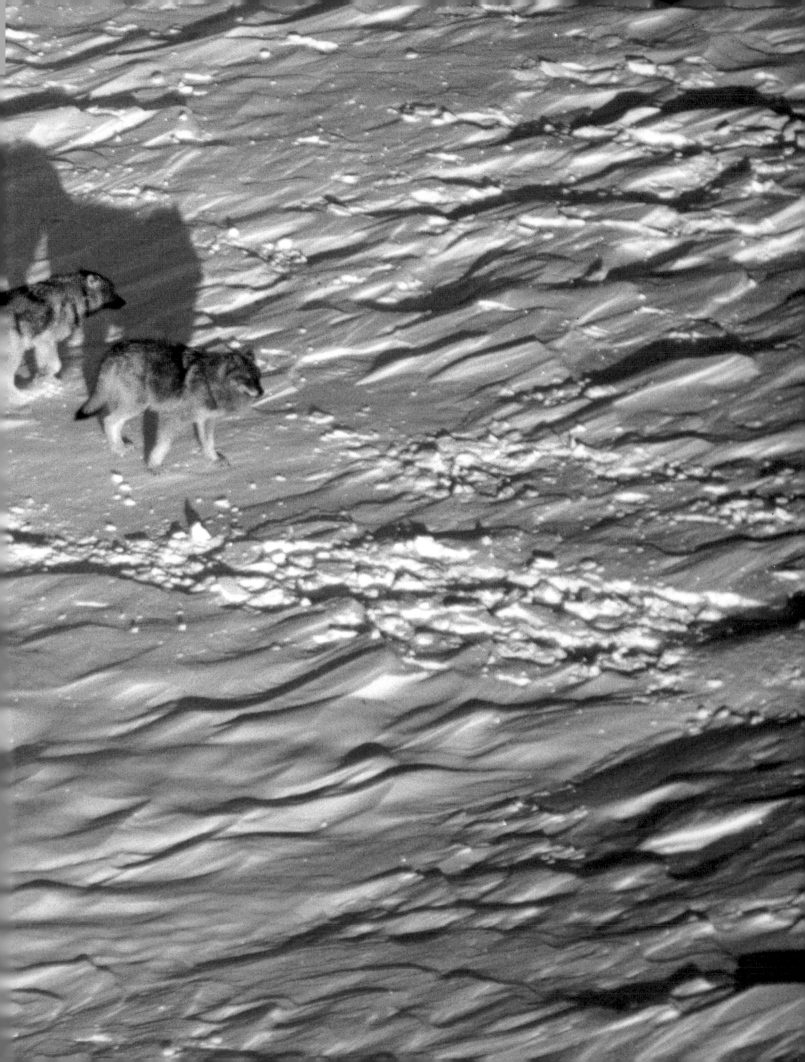

CHAPTER 1

Historical Overview of Minnesota Wolf Recovery
by L. David Mech

It is perhaps fitting that the first wolves I ever saw in Minnesota were from an aircraft piloted by a wolf hunter. Pilot Don Murray had flown me from the Eveleth airport northeastward over the Superior National Forest. Murray had used his keen tracking skills to lead us to the pack. There we watched a pack of seven wolves unsuccessfully chase six deer during the next hour.

This odd combination of a wolf hunter guiding a wolf biologist seemed symbolic in some way; it was 1964, and not only was aerial wolf hunting now illegal, but the wolf was about to be placed on a federal endangered species list. This flight could have been considered a type of "passing on the baton," for I was soon to be hired by the U.S. Fish and Wildlife Service to study the wolf in the Superior National Forest. The many thousands of hours I would eventually spend in small, cramped planes pursuing wolves would lead not to the creatures' demise but to the betterment of their population.

Wolf Populations Before 1965

Nobody knows how many wolves originally inhabited Minnesota. However, since wolf densities usually run about five to ten per hundred square miles (5 to 10 per 260 square km) where deer, moose, elk, and bison are prey, it seems reasonable that Minnesota's 79,617 square miles (206,208 square km) may once have held 4,000 to 8,000 wolves. Whatever the number, there were enough wolves so that, like every other state, Minnesota devoted considerable effort trying to eliminate them.

Facing page: The wolf in Minnesota has had a long and interesting history. In contrast to in most other states, the animal persisted despite intensive persecution, responded to federal protection under the Endangered Species Act, and now occupies all of Minnesota's northern wilderness and semi-wilderness. (Photograph © Alan & Sandy Carey)
Inset: A Minnesotan on his way to a county auditor with ten wolf pelts in 1916. Bounty hunters used any means to kill wolves and turned in their pelts for payments. Minnesota removed its wolf bounty in 1965 when Governor Karl Rolvaag vetoed a bounty bill that the state legislature had passed. This act represented the first step in the turnaround of public attitudes toward the wolf in Minnesota. (Photograph © Minnesota Historical Society)

To European settlers, the wolf was an animal to be feared and a fierce competitor for their livestock. Europeans brought with them to America all of their myths, legends, and fairy tales about the wolf, and these stories persist today in much of our society. Trying to pare away those fictional layers is one of the main tasks of conservationists interested in wolves. (Photograph © Michael H. Francis)

The wolf bounty was a tool used in many areas as an incentive for people to kill wolves. Bounties helped reduce wolf populations in accessible parts of Minnesota. However, their main disadvantage as a management tool is that they allowed anyone to kill wolves at any time and in any place, even when and where wolves may not have been doing damage.

As the state became increasingly settled by Europeans, wolves were exterminated from more and more of it. Since southern Minnesota was settled first, wolf ranges gradually dwindled northward; poison, year-round persecution, pup destruction, aerial hunting, and bounties (instituted in 1849) having done their job.

No systematic estimates of wolf numbers are available for most of Minnesota's history, and from 1925 to 1945, the historical accounts of population trends conflict. It is known, however, that in the late 1940s and early 1950s, the Minnesota Conservation Department (now the Department of Natural Resources or DNR), backed by public sentiment, assigned several employees to wolf control. They and the public killed an estimated 300 to 400 wolves per year from 1945 to 1952, mostly in the north and northeastern parts of the state.

Because about a third to a half of a large wolf population can be killed by humans each year without reducing the basic population, this annual take implies that 600 to 1,200 wolves were present then. Field workers of the time agreed that the population probably decreased after that, and estimates of the number of wolves that inhabited Minnesota in 1963 ranged from 350 to 700. However, later assessment concluded that there were at least 650. From 1952, when bounty records first distinguished coyotes from wolves, to the end of the bounty in 1965, an average of about 190 wolves, or about a third of the population, were killed per year, mostly in accessible areas.

The Minnesota state legislative hearings became highly contentious when reauthorization of wolf bounties was considered in the mid-1960s. State Representative Loren Rutter of northern Minnesota

A few of the thirty-eight wolves killed in the wilderness around Ely by an aerial hunter during winter 1946–47. The wolves, when caught out on open lakes, were either shot from the air or killed after the plane landed nearby. Aircraft were used because of the inaccessibility of the wilderness by other means and because of the difficulty of hunting wolves any other way.

brought a frozen wolf to the capitol steps in St. Paul for all the world to see how large its teeth were. Members of Help Our Wolves Live (HOWL), a Minneapolis-based group, countered with statistics and scientific facts about the wolf.

In 1965, Governor Karl Rolvaag vetoed the state's last bounty bill. He then lost the next election by fifty-four votes, and it is widely believed that his bounty veto cost him the election. Wolves were restricted at that time primarily to Cook, Lake, St. Louis, Koochiching, Lake of the Woods, Beltrami, and Roseau Counties.

Early Wolf Management Programs

The $35 bounty (equivalent to about $235 in 1999) and a year-round open season probably helped hold the wolf population down in accessible areas, so the removal of the bounty then allowed a gradual repopulation in those areas. In 1966, the first federal Endangered Species Act was passed, alerting the public to the problem; however, it provided no legal protection. In 1967, the wolf in Minnesota was declared endangered under this act. The Minnesota DNR estimated that some 735 to 950 wolves inhabited the state within a few years after that.

Meanwhile, the Minnesota state legislature instituted a "directed predator control program" in 1969. Trappers could be approved by local conservation officers to trap wolves on or around farms suffering depredations, and the trappers would be paid for each wolf they caught on the approved farm. This

In this 1933 photo, a game warden in the Lake Vermilion, Sioux River, and Lac La Croix areas, displays a wolf he has trapped. Wolves were so widely reviled in historic times that even government officials such as game wardens participated in the attempt to eliminate them. Using snares, traps, the digging of pups out of dens, and any other method, most outdoorsmen considered it their solemn duty to help exterminate the wolf. (Photograph © Minnesota Historical Society)

Above: With snowshoes and sled, early wolf hunters were able to travel only a few miles a day in the wilderness. They would string out a line of poison baits on open lakes and then visit them many days later to seek the results of their efforts. During mid-winter, the "wolfers" could not only claim a bounty for any wolf killed, but they might also sell its pelt. (Photograph © Minnesota Historical Society)

Right: Wolves poisoned along the Lake Superior shore in the late 1960s during controversy over attempts to reinstate the bounty. Poisoning was the primary method used to exterminate wolves throughout the United States because it was far more effective and efficient than hunting or trapping. Poisoning is still used to control wolves in parts of Canada. (Photograph from the collection of L. David Mech)

As the persecution of wolves in agricultural and semi-wilderness areas took its toll, the main places where relatively intact packs of wolves survived were in the most inaccessible wilderness areas. Such packs acted as reservoirs, so when the bounty was removed and pressure on wolves loosened, dispersing wolves from these packs helped repopulate neighboring areas. (Photograph © D. Robert Franz)

program accounted for the elimination of eighteen to ninety-two wolves per year, depending on how many depredations there were and how successful the trappers were.

Although the Directed Wolf Control Program was subject to abuse, it did generally tend to take wolves inhabiting the more accessible parts of wolf range. Thus, wolves remained restricted primarily to wilderness, particularly the Superior National Forest and surroundings in northeastern Minnesota. At the same time, the new state program meant that wolves in semi-wilderness and not preying on livestock also bore less pressure.

Of course, the program did not work perfectly. A wolf I radioed in the Superior National Forest was killed there, then sold to a fur buyer eighty miles (129 km) west. It then ended up being turned in for payment at a farm another eighty miles farther west. The predator controller had bought the wolf from the fur buyer and then claimed he caught it at the farm. The only trouble was he forgot to remove the ear tags. When the game warden asked where I tagged the wolf, I also told him where it had been killed. The controller was convicted.

Wolves could still be killed year-round anywhere in the state, so hunters and trappers took them while hunting or trapping other game. However, there was no special incentive to kill wolves if they were not preying on livestock, so the pressure was off. Slowly, the wolf population began to respond.

The Comeback and Its Costs

Wolves may disperse up to hundreds of miles as they mature. Thus, the wilderness population, including those in Canada, became a reservoir for wolves to continue to recolonize semi-wilderness areas along the western and southern edge of their Minnesota range as they had been wiped out there.

Even as early as 1970, a breeding pack of wolves inhabited the Hill City area in Aitkin County. In the northwestern part of Minnesota, wolves also began to make a comeback, and a few animals were also

In 1970, Superior National Forest supervisor Craig Rupp issued an order prohibiting the taking of wolves on federal land within the Superior National Forest. However, on the state land in the Superior National Forest and elsewhere throughout Minnesota, wolves could still be killed anywhere at any time by almost any means. (Photograph © L. David Mech)

Even though wolves were legally protected starting in August 1974 by the Endangered Species Act of 1973, some are still killed illegally. It is impossible to accurately estimate the number so taken, for usually it is only if the wolf is radio-tagged that the cause of its fate is known. (Photograph © Steven H. Fritts)

killed in Pine County near Wisconsin. This positive momentum was given a major boost by the federal Endangered Species Act of 1973, which legally protected the Minnesota wolf as of August 1974.

The public uproar in wolf range, however, was instant and widespread. Wolf carcasses were left on courthouse steps in International Falls. Meetings about the issue turned to shouting matches. In response to a cattleman's statement that wolf lovers should put their money where their mouth is and help pay for cattle lost to wolves, one wolf lover stood with her hands on her hips, and instantly retorted "Put your brains where your mouth is," and sat down.

A degree of federal protection had already been granted the wolf in 1970 in the Superior National Forest, partly because of my research. One of the first wolves that I had radio-tagged there, Wolf 1075, was caught by a fur trapper who then reported it to me. Luckily, I knew the trapper was operating there and had told him of my valuable animal, so he had not killed it. I then paid the trapper $100 (1970 dollars) out of my pocket, and he allowed me to turn the wolf loose with a new radio.

Some question remained about whether or not I would have to pay a second fee if the trapper recaptured the wolf, but that wasn't very likely. When the same trapper caught a wolf radioed by another researcher, this became too much for the U.S. Forest Service, on whose land we were all working. Forest Supervisor Craig Rupp issued a special order protecting wolves on all federal land within the boundaries of the Superior National Forest. But to this day, even after they were granted total federal protection in 1974, wolves from the forest continue to be killed illegally.

Most illegal wolf killing occurs during deer-hunting season when 100,000 to 200,000 deer hunters are afield in wolf range. By chance, every now and then, wolves run by hunters, some of whom shoot them. In the past, such an animal became a trophy. Since it became illegal, the animals are often just left. Thus there is little way to know the present extent of this problem.

At times, coyote or fox trappers also accidentally catch wolves. Most often they either release the animal or call a conservation officer to help them release it. But occasionally trappers will shoot the wolf and leave it in the woods. Again, it is difficult to know how often this occurs.

Although the number of wolves killed illegally is

Dispersing wolves from the Minnesota wilderness and even from the adjoining Ontario wilderness traveled far and wide seeking mates and new places to live in regions where wolves had been extirpated. Those heading south and west out of northeastern Minnesota eventually helped found new populations that began to recolonize suitable areas. (Photograph © Michael H. Francis)

unknown, that number has not been enough to stop the growth of the Minnesota wolf population. A human take of 30 to 50 percent of the population each year would be necessary to limit the population. The combination of wolves killed by the federal depredation control program (see chapter 8) and whatever illegal killing there is hardly has come close to that figure.

Wolves Continue to Thrive

Public attitudes towards wolves and wolf protection have changed dramatically since the early 1970s. Dr. Steven Kellert of Yale University found that by 1999 about 80 percent of Minnesota hunters and trappers looked positively on the wolf. Eighty-three percent of hunters and 78 percent of trappers agreed with the statement "The presence of wolves adds a great deal to the Minnesota wilderness experience" (see chapter 8).

This change in attitude probably reflects both the loss of an older generation who harbored strong anti-wolf feelings and its replacement by a younger generation more knowledgeable about wolves and other wildlife and environmental issues.

Thus, in the early 1970s, with the bounty gone and legal protection increasing, the Minnesota wolf population began to expand its range. Besides the pack of wolves occupying the Hill City area, another pack or packs sprang up in the Nemadji State Forest area along the Minnesota/Wisconsin border north of Hinckley. By 1975, wolves had made their way back into Wisconsin. From 1975 through 1979, four wolves were killed in Wisconsin within seventeen miles (27 km) of Minnesota. Furthermore, biologists in Wisconsin were finding other evidence of wolves recolonizing the state.

Although it might seem most logical that the Wisconsin wolf population resulted from dispersing

Figure 1

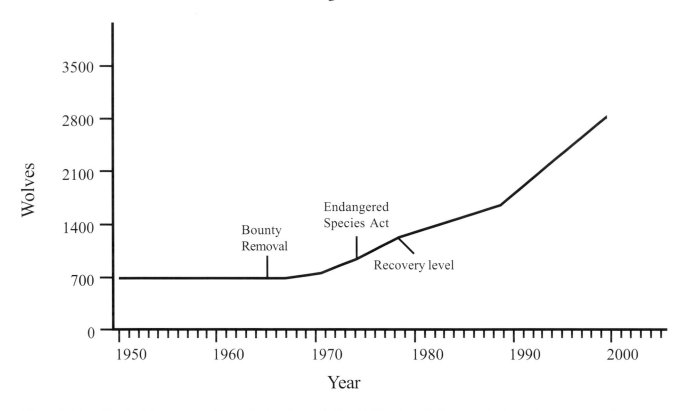

Figure 1: Trend in the Minnesota wolf population from 1970 to 1997, when the last population estimate was made. Increase represents range expansion. Density in most local areas where the wolf lived in 1970 has not increased (see Figure 2). (Data: Minnesota Department of Natural Resources)

animals from the Nemadji State Forest or Hill City packs or other unknown packs south of Duluth, the animals that recolonized Wisconsin could have come from almost anywhere in Minnesota or even Ontario. Wolves sometimes disperse distances of more than 500 miles (805 km), and tagged wolves originating near Ely and Isabella in northeastern Minnesota have ended up in southern Wisconsin north of Madison and in northern Michigan.

By 1978, some 1,250 wolves inhabited Minnesota, and they clearly were responding well to protection (Figure 1). A wolf recovery team appointed by the U.S. Fish and Wildlife Service concluded that this was the optimal number of wolves for the state. The team also recommended that the Minnesota wolf be reclassified from endangered to threatened, which the federal government did in 1978. This classification allowed more flexible management, including lethal government control of wolves preying on livestock.

I was then assigned to set up and direct the depredation-control program in addition to my research

duties. This program was not to be a wolf-population-control measure—only an attempt to respond to the wolf's killing of livestock case by case in order to minimize further losses. In addition, Minnesota began paying compensation to farmers who sustained livestock losses to wolves (see chapter 8).

In northwestern Minnesota, wolves quickly filled vacant habitat in the Beltrami Island State Forest south of Warroad. Wolves from northern Minnesota continued to disperse into Wisconsin and Michigan and into areas of Minnesota where they had not lived for many years. A wolf we radioed near Ely ended up south of Mille Lacs Lake in central Minnesota, for example; a few years later at least one pack was resident in that area and was producing pups. Other dispersing wolves were struck by cars or shot when mistaken for coyotes even farther south. By 1989, the Minnesota DNR estimated that some 1,500 to 1,750 wolves inhabited Minnesota.

In 1994, reproducing wolves were documented just north of the town of Milaca and in the Minnesota Army National Guard Camp Ripley Training

Figure 2

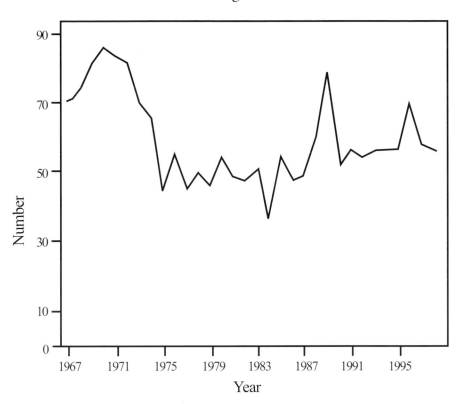

Figure 2: Trend in wolf density of the central Superior National Forest from 1968 to 1999. (Data: L. David Mech, Biological Resources Division, U.S. Geological Survey)

Site northwest of St. Cloud. A wolf radioed by the Wisconsin Department of Natural Resources in St. Croix State Park east of Hinckley, Minnesota, dispersed southward to the town of Hugo just nineteen miles north of the center of St. Paul. The animal hung around Hugo and nearby Forest Lake for a few weeks, then returned north and eventually settled in Wisconsin.

Similarly, wolves continued to push their Minnesota range westward and southward, as indicated by their depredations on livestock in new areas each year. By the mid-1990s, a pack had established itself in an area within twenty miles (32 km) of Moorhead, along the Minnesota border with North Dakota, and in 1997 a pair of wolves inhabited the Elk River area just northwest of the Twin Cities. Other wolves were killed accidentally in Rochester and just west and north of the Twin Cities in 1998 and 1999.

The Future: The Challenges of Success
No one knows how much of Minnesota wolves might eventually repopulate. That will depend at least partly on the state regulations governing the killing of wolves as well as on public attitudes. Because the wolf's only biological requirement is sufficient food, usually in the form of hoofed animals, these carnivores could inhabit most of Minnesota, for deer are available throughout the state.

By winter 1997–98, the wolf population had recovered enough in Wisconsin, Michigan, and Minnesota that the species had become eligible for removal from the federal endangered species list ("delisted"). A new Minnesota DNR systematic estimate showed that Minnesota supported about 2,500 wolves in winter of 1997–98, and that they and their range are increasing 4.5 percent per year (Figure 1). (It is important to understand that most of the wolf increase is resulting from range expansion. In any given area of the wolf's long-established range, the wolf density has fluctuated over the years, but in most of that area there has been no net increase [Figure 2].)

In addition to Minnesota's expanding wolf population, Wisconsin and Michigan (excluding Isle

By the early 1990s, wolves had recovered so well in Minnesota that they had recolonized Camp Ripley in central Minnesota, and individual wolves had reached the Twin Cities' suburbs. Milaca is the town nearest to the Twin Cities where a wolf pair is known to have successfully bred. (Photograph © D. Robert Franz)

Royale in Lake Superior) now hold some 400 wolves. At this writing, the process of delisting wolves in all three states is underway. When delisted, wolves will be managed by the individual states.

As wolves colonize more agricultural land, they tend also to kill more livestock and pets, thus incensing rural residents. This killing generally leads to increased animosity toward wolves, more government depredation control, and more wolves killed. However, it remains to be seen whether budgets and personnel can be increased fast enough to service all the depredation complaints brought by the burgeoning wolf population. The current annual expense of each individual wolf outside the wilderness area is very high. Even with conservative assumptions, wolf depredation control and compensation for damages costs taxpayers about $200 per wolf every year for each of the 1,100 wolves living outside the wilderness, as well as about $90 for each wilderness wolf.

One possible solution to the increasing cost of wolves would be to try to control the wolf population expansion or to actually reduce the population. However, this possibility seems remote. The main way wolves were controlled and exterminated originally was through widespread poisoning and aerial hunting. They are very hard to hunt or trap systematically, and there is little incentive for enough hunters and trappers to do so. Each of Minnesota's estimated 350 to 400 packs would produce an average of five to six pups each year. To reduce the Minnesota population would require killing 1,000 to 2,000 wolves each year, for that is the population's potential annual increase.

Because of the change in human attitudes towards wolves during the last two decades, no doubt any human taking of wolves would be highly regulated, as it is with other species. It would be reasonable to focus any public harvesting where wolves are causing the most damage to livestock and pets. If enough wolves could be taken, this harvest would tend to restrict wolves mainly to the less accessible areas of the state. Most of these areas probably would be northeast of a line between about Pine City and the northwest corner of Minnesota.

Attempts at a New Management Plan

Before the federal government will delist the wolf and return management back to Minnesota, it insists that the state develop an adequate management plan.

Minnesotans, however, are highly polarized about how the state should manage its wolves. About half of the public wants them restricted to the wilderness or at least their present range, while the other half thinks they should be allowed to live all over the state.

To try to devise a plan that might be acceptable to most people, the Minnesota DNR held a series of public meetings in early 1998 and then assembled a "wolf stakeholders roundtable." The roundtable consisted of thirty-three members representing various vested interests, including hunters and trappers; animal rights and wildlife conservation groups; American Indian tribes; farmers and livestock owners; and residents and property owners from areas in wolf range. They believed that if they reached consensus on a management plan, the state legislature would accept their consensus, and the federal government would delist the wolf.

Amid tears, anger, and frustration, hours after the official adjournment time on the last of eight days of discussions, the roundtable more or less agreed to a consensus. Essentially, the agreement was to protect the wolf population for at least another five years after delisting. However, roundtable members never did sign the final agreement; in 1999, the state legislature also rejected it but failed to devise a plan of its own.

The Endangered Species Act itself does not require a management plan for the federal government to be able to delist the wolf. It requires only that the government be assured that the species will not be threatened with endangerment again. That assurance has certainly been met in Minnesota. The U.S. Fish and Wildlife Service's recovery team recommended that Minnesota needs 1,250 wolves to assure recovery. Twice as many wolves now inhabit Minnesota. The wolves are protected by Minnesota law; poisoning wolves and aerial hunting are banned. Because there is no practical way wolf numbers could be reduced below recovery level (see chapter 8), the recovery team advised in 1999 that the wolf be delisted as soon as possible.

Nevertheless, the U.S. Fish and Wildlife Service, apparently fearing a lawsuit from wildlife preservationists, declined to delist the wolf. At this writing in early 2000, the Minnesota DNR has developed its own wolf management plan. The DNR hopes that the state legislature will approve the plan during 2000, so that the federal government will then delist the wolf and the Minnesota DNR can resume managing the state's wolf population.

How ever Minnesota finally decides to manage its wolves, it will never please everyone. The best that can be hoped for is a reasonably cost-effective plan that will maintain the wolf population at least in wilderness areas while minimizing conflict with humans. Such a plan would reduce public animosity towards and illegal persecution of the wolf. As one prominent Minnesota cattleman says, "We don't want to exterminate wolves. Let them live all they want in the wilderness. But please let us protect our own property from them."

Facing page, top: According to Minnesota Department of Natural Resources estimates, in winter 1997–98, 350 to 400 packs of wolves inhabited Minnesota. If producing the usual average number of pups each year, these packs would add about 2,000 new wolves annually. Such high productivity in such a large population now makes it difficult, if not impossible, to control wolf numbers. (Photograph © L. David Mech)

Facing page, bottom: Now biologically well recovered in Minnesota, the wolf fosters a variety of feelings and attitudes among the public. Attitudes run the gamut from outright hatred of the wolf to adoration, although most people's view are far more moderate. Nevertheless, trying to get people with strong feelings about the wolf to agree on a management plan has been a trying exercise for government officials. (Photograph © Alan & Sandy Carey)

CHAPTER 2

Minnesota Wolf Range: Past, Present, and Future
by Robert R. Ream

On November 27, 1968, I saw my first wild wolf. It was in a live-trap in the Boundary Waters Canoe Area Wilderness (BWCAW), the wolf's last stronghold in Minnesota. Dave Mech and

trapper Bob Himes couldn't have been happier, for we had been checking Himes's trapline for three weeks, and we finally had connected. Mech, with his usual careful attention to detail, placed a radio collar on this wolf—the first wolf in the United States to receive such a collar. I then spent many memorable hours in an airplane that winter radio-tracking this and four other wolves. In the thirty years since, Mech has followed these wolves and their offspring, more than 700 animals in total, and the scientific world has been enriched with the knowledge gained.

Ten years earlier, I had canoed this wilderness for ten days with college friends. Having grown up on a farm in southern Wisconsin, the Boundary Waters was a magical place that I had only heard and read about in Aldo Leopold and Sigurd Olson's writings. Now I was back here holding a real live wolf while Mech fitted the collar!

During the ten years between my first visit to the area and that cold winter day, the Wilderness Act passed (1964), making the BWCAW one of the first nine congressionally mandated wilderness areas in the United States. A ban on aircraft use below 4,000 feet (1,219 m) over the BWCAW was also in effect, thus ending aerial wolf hunting in that area, although not in the surroundings. I remember visiting stores in Ely, when I first started working as a

Facing page: Minnesota wolf range, while once restricted to pristine wilderness, has now expanded to cover agricultural land and other habitats. However, as human development continues throughout the state, it may only be in such pristine areas where wolves will be able to live without conflict with humans. (Photograph © Fred H. Harrington)
Inset: Wolves can live in any kind of habitat in the northern hemisphere where there is enough food, usually hoofed animals. Because such type of prey frequent all kinds of habitat, so too can wolves. Historically, Minnesota wolves occupied prairies, brushland, oak forests, river bottoms, and the northern boreal forests. Only because they were restricted by persecution to the northern wilderness have they come to be thought of as northern forest animals. (Photograph © Michael H. Francis)

Figure 3

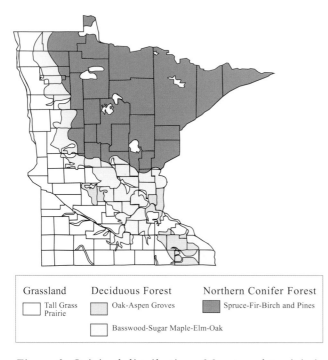

Grassland
- Tall Grass Prairie

Deciduous Forest
- Oak-Aspen Groves
- Basswood-Sugar Maple-Elm-Oak

Northern Conifer Forest
- Spruce-Fir-Birch and Pines

Figure 3: Original distribution of forest and prairie in Minnesota. (Data source: Minnesota Department of Natural Resources)

U.S. Forest Service research biologist in 1966, and seeing postcards of a ski plane on a frozen BWCAW lake with numerous frozen wolves propped in front of the plane, presumably shot from the air.

By 1968, the BWCAW, a few areas around it, and nearby Isle Royale National Park were the only places in the entire lower forty-eight states with wolf populations. And here wilderness designation and the air ban were the only things preventing their demise. When we first started aerial radio-tracking that winter, some wolves would bolt for cover if found on a frozen lake, apparently associating aircraft with aerial gunning. It would be another five years before the Endangered Species Act of 1973 would be passed and another year for the act to take effect in Minnesota.

Diverse Habitats, Abundant Wildlife

Before European settlers arrived, wolves lived throughout Minnesota, both in the prairies of southwestern Minnesota and the forests of the north. As far as habitat is concerned, the wolf is capable of living anywhere there are hoofed animals—forest, prairie, mountains, desert, tundra, swamps, or barren ground. That is why the creature was originally the world's most widely distributed land mammal.

Shaped by natural forces such as fire and continental glaciers, Minnesota was, and still is, a land with a great diversity of habitats and abundant wildlife.

In the area that is now southwestern Minnesota, early European explorers rode through the prairies with thick grasses reaching the bellies of their horses. The deep-rooted prairie plants had built up deep, rich soils over thousands of years. Elk, deer, and even bison occupied the fertile plains and provided prey for the abundant wolves in the area. The explorers observed Native Americans setting fire to the prairies in the spring to remove the old growth. The blackened surface warmed the soil and provided lush new green growth that attracted grazing animals for their hunters as much as a month earlier than the unburned areas. In the hilly country of southeastern Minne-

Facing page, top: When wolves originally inhabited southern Minnesota, they had multitudes of deer, elk, and bison on which to prey. The rich soils of prairie and plains grew an abundance of wildlife. Now due to changes wrought by European settlers, these areas have become farmland, and only the white-tailed deer remain as wild prey for any wolves that happen to repopulate such areas. (Photograph © Bill Marchel)

Facing page, bottom: Shallow lakes and extensive spruce bogs characterize much of northwestern and north central Minnesota. Here caribou and moose used to live, but only moose remain. Along with deer in the uplands, moose form the main part of the wolf's diet in such areas. Proposals to restore caribou to the area have stalled. (Photograph © Layne Kennedy)

Northeastern Minnesota's large expanse of boreal and mixed deciduous forest forms thick protective cover for wolves and other wildlife. It is laden with many rare and interesting species, including, besides wolves and their prey, fisher, marten, bobcats, and even the occasional lynx. Nevertheless, because of the forest's thickness and impenetrability, these creatures are seldom seen. (Photograph © Layne Kennedy)

sota, prairies dominated the ridges, with forests in the more moist and sheltered valleys.

Along the prairie-forest border extended a gradual transition zone from grasslands to forest, providing ideal habitat for large mammals, such as white-tailed deer and elk, that could graze on the prairies and retreat into forest for cover. Along the southern part of this transition were oak savannas (scattered bur oaks in prairie). In the northern part of the transition zone, aspen parklands prevailed, with clumps of aspen extending into the prairies.

The "Big Woods" of central Minnesota, south, west, and northwest of what is now the sprawling Twin Cities, was mostly hardwood or mixed hardwood-conifer forest that supported numerous white-tailed deer.

Much of north-central and northwestern Minnesota was leveled by glaciers and covered by glacial Lake Aggasiz following the last period of glaciation. Shallow lakes and extensive areas of black spruce bogs, reminiscent of the muskeg of Canada, cover this area

even today. Moose occupied most of this region and were probably the main prey for wolves there, although some of Minnesota's last caribou also lived there. Because of the poor, wet soils, human settlements were few and far between, and road densities were low. This was the last part of Minnesota to be settled by Europeans.

A massive but unsuccessful effort was once mounted in the northwestern bog country to drain the area and convert it to agricultural land. A widespread system of old drainage ditches is a present reminder of that bygone era.

In the northeast corner of Minnesota, or the "Arrowhead" country, glaciers scraped down to bedrock leaving stria, or long scratches, visible on exposed bedrock. Reminding one of the tundra far to the north, the barren areas are still covered with *Cladonia* lichens, popularly known as "reindeer moss," a staple food of woodland caribou. This is still the land of the boreal conifer forests, as it was hundreds of years ago.

On shallower upland soils, jackpines, perpetuated by intense forest fires, dominated the landscape. Red and white pine stands—mixed with aspen, red maple, and other hardwoods—occupied the deeper upland soils. Where glaciers scoured out deep depressions, they left behind numerous lakes, while shallower depressions filled in with peat moss, black spruce, and tamarack. Moose and woodland caribou were more numerous than deer prior to European settlement and were major prey species for wolves there. Beavers were abundant in early successional stages following forest fires, and deer moved in after the widespread logging and burning.

Settlers vs. Wolves

The rich prairie soils of the south were the first to be plowed by the European settlers starting in the 1840s. Many of these settlers came from Scandinavian countries where wolves still existed. They feared wolves and worried about their livestock, so like their neighbors in other states, they waged war on the wolves. "The only good wolf is a dead wolf" was their motto.

By 1900, wolves were rare in the agricultural areas of southern and western Minnesota. Settlement proceeded from the south northward as the prairie-forest transition and the Big Woods fell to the settlers' axes, converting forest to farmland. Game laws were few and generous, and deer and elk succumbed to the guns of settlers and market hunters. These native prey were then replaced by domestic livestock.

Meanwhile, cities grew rapidly throughout the Midwest, accompanied by an increased demand for lumber. Lumber companies moved from northern Wisconsin into the Big Woods of Minnesota as the supplies dwindled in Wisconsin. Settlers quickly followed into the cutover lands and started farming. Logging then proceeded to the northeast corner of Minnesota, and from 1890 to the 1920s, the great majestic stands of virgin red and white pines yielded to the axe and the forest fires that accompanied logging.

Even a third of the area now known as the BWCAW was cut over during this era. The days of Paul Bunyan in the Great Lakes forests dramatically changed the landscape and ecology of the area. Logging, settlement, and other development continued to the present time but at a much slower rate. Following World War II, logging and logging roads pervaded another third of the present BWCAW. Along with the intensive exploitation of the forests

The moose is one of the Minnesota wolf's main prey animals, just below the white-tailed deer in importance. In the east-central Superior National Forest, especially in the eastern Boundary Waters Canoe Area Wilderness, moose are the only prey animals available to wolves year-round. In summer, wolves can also take beavers, and an occasional deer strays there just for the season. (Photograph © Bill Marchel)

Figure 4

Figure 4: Expansion of the wolf range in Minnesota from 1977 to 1999. (Data: Minnesota Department of Natural Resources)

naturally came the persecution of predators, especially the wolf. Carnivores had to be eliminated, because they were widely regarded as competitors with humans. Logging roads allowed the access to the wolves.

Prey populations for wolves and other predators probably reached a low in Minnesota in the 1920s. Then a combination of strict wildlife conservation laws, passed in response to public concern about dwindling wildlife populations, and very favorable deer habitat, created by second-growth forests, produced a rapid rise in deer populations. Deer numbers reached levels that were probably higher than those prior to European settlement. However, because wolves were seen as a hindrance to deer population growth, wolf persecution continued in accessible parts of the wilderness.

Wolves Reclaim Their Territory

The turnaround in the wolf population (detailed in chapter 1) allowed the wolf to begin repopulating areas of Minnesota where the animal had not lived in over a century (see Figure 4). During this time, of course, bison and elk were supplanted by cattle and sheep. Wagon trails became highways, and sparse farmsteads multiplied by orders of magnitude.

But the wolf is adaptable. It can live on cattle instead of bison. Back roads can be convenient wolf trails. Even interstate highways are no impediment. And wheat or cornfields are as good a place to hide as prairies.

The question Minnesotans are now faced with is how much of the agricultural part of the wolf's former range are they going to let the wolf re-take? The issue is complicated by the attitudes of the public, which is about equally divided between those favoring wolf recolonization of all of Minnesota and those believing the wolf should be restricted to the non-agricultural areas.

With poisoning of protected animals no longer legal, however, there seems to be little humans can do to control the Minnesota wolf population. Thus, it might be the wolf, rather than the public, that will decide how much of the state it will re-occupy.

Facing page, top: Logging roads were once the bane of the wolf in the northern forests because they allowed accessibility to people interested in wiping out the wolves. However, once wolves were protected, similar roads and the logging they brought yielded a flush of deer that helped wolf populations increase and furthered their recovery. (Photograph © Layne Kennedy)
Facing page, bottom: How can wolves and humans live together? Is the better approach to allow wolves to inhabit only wilderness where they conflict least with humans, as many people propose? Or is there some way wolves can live among people without fostering ill feelings by killing pets and livestock and instilling fear for the safety of children, as others believe? (Photograph © D. Robert Franz)

CHAPTER 3

Wolf Research in Minnesota
by L. David Mech

The Footsteps of Sigurd Olson

Sigurd Olson is one of Minnesota's most famous citizens. He distinguished himself as one of the earliest wilderness proponents and wilderness writers. While his career was developing, Olson paid some of science's earliest attention to the wolf. Science is self-correcting. Our knowledge progresses from gross general notions about how things work to more and more specific, and generally more accurate, ideas as research continues. Olson helped start the research process with the wolf. Until his field studies in the late 1930s, few, if any, articles had been published about the wolf in scientific journals. Most information about the wolf was restricted to general texts about mammals or wildlife, such as those by Ernest Thompson Seton and others.

As a young student, Olson at first thought Seton had learned all there was to know about the wolf. But after his advisor cautioned that "no one's work stands alone," he decided that he would indeed study the wolf for his master's degree.

So Olson donned his snowshoes in the Superior National Forest and tracked wolves. In this way, he gained a feel for the way wolves traveled and made their way through the wilderness. He then wrote up his insights, publishing them in the scientific journal *Ecology*.

Olson no doubt found that wolves are not easy to study for several reasons. They live in relatively low densities, which makes them difficult to find. Whereas deer are usually measured in number (as many as twenty-five) per square mile (per 2.6 square km), wolves are

Facing page: Radio-tracking from the air and the ground has revolutionized wolf research. Radio-collars allow each wolf to be identified consistently and located at nearly any time. These two important advantages further allow biologists to collect many other types of data on such subjects as survival, mortality, reproduction, scent-marking, howling, and spatial organization of the wolf population. (Photograph © Layne Kennedy)
Inset: By following wolf tracks for many miles, Olson gained a feel for the wolf's ways and set the stage for generations of wolf biologists to follow with higher-tech methods. (Photograph by Eugene D. Becker, © Minnesota Historical Society)

The snowy woods of northern Minnesota have changed little since Sigurd Olson trekked through them on snowshoes in the late 1930s. Many generations of wolves have inhabited these forests since Olson's time, and gradually over the years they have yielded the secrets of their lives to biologists who have followed in Olson's footsteps. (Photograph © Layne Kennedy)

measured in number per 100 square miles (per 260 square km). Wolves also travel far and wide, another reason why they are hard to study. They can tread readily through heavily forested, snow-covered areas, but humans cannot. Wolves may travel thirty miles (48 km) in a day, but Sigurd Olson on snowshoes in the same country could only cover a few miles.

Because wolves have been persecuted for so long, they tend to avoid humans and don't often remain where they can be observed. For instance, I hiked 1,500 miles (2,414 km) on Isle Royale in Lake Superior and caught only glimpses of three wolves. Thus, watching wolves directly is almost out of the question. Following their tracks in the snow, then, becomes a necessity, even though it is difficult, time consuming, grueling, and very inefficient. Only the dim, cloudy outlines of wolf behavior and activity can be derived from such studies, and the cost is great relative to the payoff. Thus, Olson did the best he could with the means available, and it was a valiant effort.

Other Early Scientific Attention

After Olson's snowshoe-based studies in northeastern Minnesota, the wolf gained a bit more scientific attention, particularly in the mid-1940s. Stanley Young and Edward Goldman, biologists for the U.S. Fish and Wildlife Service, assembled the available historical and technical information about the wolf into a useful reference work, *The Wolves of North America*. This book became the bible for anyone interested in the wolf. Much of the material in the book, however, was based on historical notes and accounts, which may be unreliable.

Also appearing in 1944 was Adolph Murie's monograph, *The Wolves of Mt. McKinley*, based on Murie's direct observations of wolves in Alaska's Mount McKinley National Park (now Denali National Park). There, because the area was far more open than Minnesota, wolves could be watched from a distance via binoculars and telescopes. Furthermore, the park wolves were not as persecuted as those elsewhere, so Murie had a pack he could study for more than a year. His work stands as a classic, and later studies did not so much correct Murie's work as they did refine it and fill in more details.

After the seminal year of 1944, when Murie and Young and Goldman published their major works, through the late 1950s, only a few wolf studies were

Milton H. ("Milt") Stenlund, a graduate student at the University of Minnesota, decided to study wolves in the Boundary Waters Canoe Area Wilderness for his master's degree. After doing field work from 1946 to 1952, Stenlund authored the booklet, "A Field Study of the Timber Wolf (Canis lupus) *on the Superior National Forest, Minnesota." (Photograph by Bryan Stenlund, © Milt Stenlund)*

conducted anywhere. Most of these were Canadian projects, because Canada was where most of the wolves were. By 1955, the United States had pretty well wiped out its wolves from most of the forty-eight contiguous states except Minnesota. A few wolves still held out in northern Michigan and Wisconsin at that time, but their days were numbered.

Milt Stenlund Studies Wolves from the Air

North of Michigan and Wisconsin, wolves had made it across the Lake Superior ice from Ontario in 1949 to Isle Royale National Park, a 210-square-mile (544-square-km) island fifteen to twenty miles (24 to 32 km) from the Ontario-Minnesota border. These wolves had gained some attention and were being investigated by the National Park Service. Later Purdue University would launch the world's best-known wolf study there.

Two of Minnesota's aerial wolf hunters became research pilots for the Isle Royale wolf-moose study. Since they were already skilled at tracking wolves from the air, they were a great asset to the project.

Because aerial tracking was one of the few ways anyone could actually find wolves, this technique would eventually be used by biologists to study wolves. One of the first to take advantage of this technique was a young graduate student at the University of Minnesota, Milt Stenlund.

Stenlund decided to study the wolves of the Superior National Forest, including the BWCAW, for his master's degree. Enlisting the help of the Minnesota Department of Natural Resources (DNR) conservation officer-pilots, U.S. Forest Service pilots, and even private pilots, Stenlund put together their tracking information, collected wolf scats, and examined carcasses of wolves killed for bounty from 1948 through 1953. His Minnesota DNR bulletin "A Field Study of the Wolf in the Superior National Forest," published in 1955, became the first major U.S. wolf study since Murie's.

Stenlund's booklet documented much important information about the wolf in Minnesota at a time when its population was reaching an all-time low. He concluded: "The timber wolf is an integral part of these wilderness areas and a reasonable population should be maintained. It is not only a major component of the ecological community, but as the recreational value of this unique area increases, the howl of the timber wolf will continually remind visitors that this lake country of the Superior National Forest is wild country—wilderness country—remaining today much the same as it existed during the era of the French Voyageur some 200 years ago."

Minnesota Wolves Pique Scientific Curiosity

For ten more years Minnesotans continued to hunt their wolf population and collect their bounties. Of course most of the wolves taken for bounty were from the most accessible areas of the state. Thus, the regions where most of the wolves remained were the most inaccessible wilderness areas, where Stenlund studied them.

Meanwhile the folks in nearby Wisconsin and Michigan had eliminated their wolf populations, except for those wolves on Isle Royale; wolves in Wisconsin and mainland Michigan were history by 1960 and 1970 respectively. The Isle Royale wolves continued to thrive because of their isolation and protection by the National Park Service.

Dr. Durward L. Allen of Purdue University, who was renowned for his book *Our Wildlife Legacy*, with great foresight assigned a series of graduate students and post-doctoral fellows to study the wolves and moose on Isle Royale. I was privileged to be Allen's first student and began the study in 1958. Still underway and currently very ably directed by Dr. Rolf Peterson of Michigan Technological University, the study remains the longest ever predator-prey investigation and possibly the longest investigation of any vertebrate population.

The Isle Royale study is relevant to the Minnesota wolf research not only because the wolves that colonized Isle Royale no doubt came from the northeastern Minnesota–southwestern Ontario wolf population, but also because it sparked my personal interest in Minnesota's wolves and led to my research.

When I flew to Isle Royale for my first winter's work, I chartered aircraft from Eveleth, Minnesota. These aircraft flew across northeastern Minnesota's Superior National Forest to the shore of Lake Superior and then across to Isle Royale. Thus, each winter from 1958 through 1961, I looked down upon the frozen lakes dotting the Superior National Forest and wondered about the lives of the wolves below.

As I learned more and more about the wolves on Isle Royale, I increasingly wondered how the wolf population on the mainland was organized. The wolves on the island were using its entire area, including the shoreline. If mainland wolves had neigh-

Milt Stenlund, a decade after Sigurd Olson, pioneered the use of aircraft to study wolves. Because of the long distances wolves travel, tracking them in the snow from the air—like wolf hunters did—produced much new information. (Photograph © L. David Mech)

It may take a biologist in a small aircraft hours to track down a pack of wolves traveling many miles from lake to lake. However, at the end of the trail, the biologist finds the pack itself and can then count its members. When the wolves begin to travel, the aircraft can follow from on high and watch how the wolves travel and even hunt. (Photograph © L. David Mech)

Wolf radio-collars weigh a little over a pound and transmit a "beep-beep-beep" type of signal for three to four years. Each collar is tuned to a different station (frequency), so each collared wolf can be identified. Signals from wolf radio-collars can be detected about a mile away by a receiver and antenna on the ground. However, from aircraft the signals can be heard ten to fifteen miles away depending on the altitudes of the aircraft. Radio-collars, made of tough machine belting and a well-protected module containing a tiny radio transmitter and batteries, are easily bolted around a wolf's neck. The same collar can also be used on deer. (Photograph © L. David Mech)

bors and no natural boundary like the shore of the island, how would those wolf packs live in relation to each other? The answer, I knew, lay in studying wolves in such an area as Minnesota.

Therefore, when I completed my phase of the Isle Royale studies in 1962, it was only natural that I should settle in Minnesota.

Radio-Tracking Enhances Research

The fact that Minnesota was fast becoming a pioneer in the development of a revolutionary wildlife research technique—radio-tracking—also kept the Minnesota wolf population at the center of wolf research. Until radio-tracking, there were only a few methods that could provide much information about wildlife. In Stenlund's study, for example, examination of scats and carcasses, aerial and ground tracking in the snow, and interviewing other field workers to record their observations were some of the only techniques available.

Radio-tracking changed all of this. This extremely useful technique, pioneered primarily by Illinois engineer William W. Cochran, allowed researchers to find an animal at will as well as to identify the individual. Not only did radio-tracking yield information about wolf movements and locations, but it opened up many other avenues of research.

Once the whereabouts of specific wolves or packs could be known, scientists could investigate factors such as mortality, dispersal, and predation. They could howl to specific packs under known conditions and study when the wolves replied, or they could snow track identifiable packs in known parts of their territory and determine their scent-marking rate (see chapter 5).

Combined with information about a wolf's age, sex, and condition, learned when the animal was live-trapped, the movements and pack affiliations of that animal could then be studied. Thus, if a wolf dispersed from its territory, such background information gave excellent insight into the whole concept of dispersal.

When I completed my phase of the Isle Royale wolf-moose study and moved to Minnesota, I soon began applying the newly developing field of radio-tracking to wildlife studies at Cochran's lab at the University of Minnesota. Meanwhile I tried to figure out how to start a wolf project in Minnesota. While writing my book *The Wolf* in the mid-to-late 1960s, I did some exploratory wolf research around Ely.

Above: When drugged wolves awaken, they are "none the worse for the wear." Although their movements may not be entirely normal for the next few days because of their capture and handling, the animals soon behave normally. (Photograph © L. David Mech)

Left: Once a radio-collared wolf of known age and sex rejoins its pack, the collar's signal leads biologists to the entire group, allowing an accurate count. The pack's movements and territory can then be determined over the next several years. (Photograph © L. David Mech)

Up Close and Personal:
When Wolves and Researchers Meet

Because most of the research on wolves in Minnesota during the past three decades has been based on radio-tracking, a critical part of the studies has been the live-capture of wolves in order to attach the radio-collars. Ten to twenty wolves per year are live-captured in steel-jawed foot traps modified to minimize any permanent foot injury to the wolf. When a wolf is caught, biologists, using a drug-filled syringe on the end of a long pole, stick the wolf with the drugs. (Photographs © Layne Kennedy)

Blood sampling captured wolves is an important method for learning about a wolf's physical condition, its disease history, and its genetic relationship to other wolves. From blood samples, researchers have learned that canine parvovirus is affecting the population under study in the east-central Superior National Forest, that wolves tend to mate with those not closely related, and that packs that live next to each other tend to be related.

Dave Mech prepares a hypodermic syringe to take samples from a wolf drugged for radio-collaring. Wolves remain drugged for about forty-five minutes, but can be kept asleep longer by being given booster doses. The drugs used have no lasting side effects.

Once a biologist is done measuring, weighing, radio-collaring, blood sampling, and examining a drugged wolf, he carries the animal to a safe place. By leaving the wolf far from where people can find it, lying it on its chest and away from water (where it might drown), the biologist is assured that the wolf will wake up in a few minutes and wander off safely.

Weighing wolves gives biologists insight into their condition. A heavy adult male in Minnesota will weigh over 100 pounds (45 kg) and a heavy female, over 85 pounds (39 kg). The young of the year weigh from 35 to 70 pounds (16 to 32 kg) by November. These weights are lighter than those of wolves in Canada and Alaska but heavier than of wolves from further south.

To study the age, sex, and condition of deer killed by wolves, Mech and associates originally "hitchhiked" airplane rides around the wilderness with state and federal pilots patrolling the area. When they found wolf-killed deer, the biologists examined the remains and collected specimens. (Photograph © L. David Mech)

Eventually that research turned into a study of the age, sex, and condition of white-tailed deer killed by wolves, which I conducted with Dr. Dan Frenzel of Macalester College in St. Paul.

On Isle Royale, the wolves killed mainly calf moose and old moose, just as the wolves Murie studied in Mount McKinley Park killed the youngest and oldest of the Dall sheep in that area. I wanted to see if the same applied to wolves killing deer. Deer were one of the smallest of the wolf's prey, and even full grown, healthy adults seemed no match for a wolf pack. Perhaps wolves could just pick off any deer, not just the fawns and oldest adults, at will.

For a few winters, Frenzel and I hitchhiked airplane rides around the Superior National Forest in Minnesota DNR and U.S. Forest Service aircraft looking for remains of wolf-killed deer. As we searched for kills, we sometimes ran across wolf packs on the frozen lakes. That burning question about how the wolf packs lived in relation to their neighbors, which I had wondered so much about while flying across Minnesota to Isle Royale, became even hotter. This time I knew how to find the answer.

Thus, in late 1968, I began live-trapping, radio-collaring, and intensively and extensively radio-tracking wolves in the central Superior National Forest—a study that continues to this day. I will never forget flying across the wilderness with a radio receiver and antennas on the wing struts and suddenly hearing the "beep-beep-beep" from the collar of my first radio-tagged wolf. A few years later, after finally learning that the wolf population was organized into pack territories (see chapter 5), I began a long-term population study as well as an investigation into anything else that could be learned about wolves from live-trapping and radio-tracking.

Since 1968, my associates and I have radioed more than 600 wolves in the population around Ely and east of it. We try to keep about a dozen contiguous wolf packs radio-tagged from year to year so we can count the population each winter and determine any changes in the territorial spacing of the packs. From the beginning, it was clear the wolves would have to be radio-tracked from aircraft, for the animals traveled too far and wide for ground tracking. On the ground, signals from radio-collars can only be heard from about a mile (1.6 km) away, whereas from an aircraft they can be heard from ten to fifteen miles (16 to 24 km).

The U.S. Department of Interior's research project in northeastern Minnesota has helped train wildlife technicians, biologists, and graduate students from around the world. Here biologists listen for a wolf radio signal with a directional antenna, trying to tell from just which direction it is coming. By repeating this procedure from another location, the scientists can tell where the wolf is by seeing where the signal bearings cross on a map. (Photograph © Layne Kennedy)

Wolf Research—and Researchers—Blossom

The use of aerial radio-tracking to study wolves ushered in a whole new era of wolf information. Interest in wolves greatly increased because of their status on the federal endangered species list. The Superior National Forest around Ely became a long-term wolf study area. Not only did it generate a wide variety of information about wolves, but it also became a training ground for future wolf biologists.

Headquartered at the U.S. Forest Service's Kawishiwi Field Lab operated by North Central Forest Experiment Station (now North Central Research Station), the joint Fish and Wildlife Service and Forest Service wolf research quickly blossomed. Technicians, graduate students, and volunteers assisted with the program and gained valuable training in wolf study techniques. I was also invited to other biologists' study areas to help them get started with live-trapping, radio-tagging, and radio-tracking wolves.

Some of the more prominent wolf biologists who received their first training in wolf study techniques on the Ely study area include Diane Boyd, Fred Harrington, Mike Nelson, Jane Packard, Bill Paul, Mike Phillips, Robert Ream, and Doug Smith. In addition, with the University of Minnesota's Dr. Elmer Birney and graduate student Steve Fritts, I began another wolf study in the Beltrami Island State Forest in northwestern Minnesota. Fritts studied the dynamics of the wolf population that was just recolonizing the area, and he eventually went on to help lead the effort to reintroduce wolves into Yellowstone National Park.

Tom Meier, John Burch, and Todd Fuller gained their first experience with wolf study techniques on Fritts's project, although over the years they also worked at Kawishiwi Field Lab. Our personnel from Kawishiwi Lab helped the Minnesota DNR start a radio-tracking study of wolves in the area south of

Grand Rapids, a study conducted by Robert Chesness, Bill Berg, and Dave Kuehn. Tom Meier also assisted the Wisconsin DNR in initiating its wolf radio-tracking study in 1979, trapping its first wolf to be radioed.

During the early years of my study, I visited Riding Mountain National Park in Manitoba and helped Lu Carbyn launch his radio-tracking investigation of wolves; the Kenai Peninsula of Alaska to set up the study in which Rolf Peterson and co-workers conducted their wolf radio-tracking; and the Abruzzo National Park in Italy where Luigi Boitani began radio-tracking wolves. One of my assistants, Steve Knick, also visited Portugal to help Francisco Fonseca begin his project there.

Thus, the Superior National Forest study area that Sigurd Olson had traversed on snowshoes in the late 1930s became a training center for wolf biologists from around the world, and it remains so to this date.

In addition, wolves have now been radio-tracked in many parts of Minnesota besides the central Superior National Forest, including the Lake Superior shore area, the Hill City area, the Minnesota-Wisconsin border, Voyageurs National Park area, the Cook-Orr area, the Bearville Study Area, Agassiz National Wildlife Refuge, the Beltrami Island region, Camp Ripley, and the Remer area. Minnesota's wolves surely are the world's most studied (see Figure 5).

Figure 5

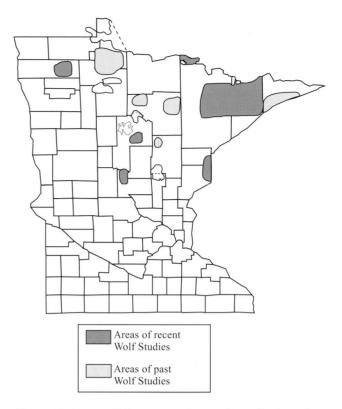

Figure 5: Areas of recent Wolf Studies

Areas of past Wolf Studies

Figure 5: Areas of Minnesota where wolf studies have been conducted since 1968. (Data: L. David Mech, Biological Resources Division, U.S. Geological Survey)

Facing page: Biologists, technicians, and trainees monitor a signal from a special capture collar. Sending a special coded signal to the collar allows them to trigger darts on the collar that drug the wolf. Obtaining experience with radio-tracking is valuable training for biologists who will work with wolves in other parts of the country and the world. (Photograph © Tom Lebovsky)

CHAPTER 4

The Minnesota Wolf
by L. David Mech

Scientific Classification

Over the years, Minnesota wolves have been known by many names, not all of them polite. Locally the animal is called the "timber wolf" to distinguish it from the coyote, which is also known as the "brush wolf." The wolf in Minnesota was long thought by scientists to belong to the race or subspecies called the eastern timber wolf (*Canis lupus lycaon*). According to the traditional scientific classification, the arbitrary line between the range of the eastern timber wolf and the range of the great plains wolf (*Canis lupus nubilus*) ran north and south through extreme western Minnesota.

Because wolves travel far and wide and sometimes disperse over 500 miles (805 km) from their birth areas, Minnesota wolves, even by the traditional classification, were probably a blend, or "intergrade," between the eastern timber wolf and the great plains wolf. Great Plains wolves came in a variety of colors, and their possible influence in Minnesota might explain why some Minnesota wolves are black and a few are even white.

The traditional classification system was probably much too liberal. It recognized twenty-four subspecies or races of wolves in North America. Given that in all of Europe and Asia, there were only eight recognized races of gray wolf, it was clear that North American wolves had fallen victim to taxonomic "splitters," or zoologists who prefer splitting a species into very fine divisions. In many cases, the wolf races in North America were based on only a single skull or skin. Considering that the widths of many of the old wolf-race ranges are less than 200 miles (322 km) across and that today's wolves are known to disperse much farther than

Facing page: The wolf that inhabits Minnesota has long been called the "timber wolf" to distinguish it from its smaller cousin, the coyote, which is often known as the "brush wolf." Scientifically, the Minnesota wolf is the gray wolf, or Canis lupus, *the same as most wolves throughout the world. The specific geographic race of wolf occupying Minnesota was thought to be the eastern timber wolf,* Canis lupus lycaon, *until about 1995. Then new studies indicated that the animal is the great plains wolf,* Canis lupus nubilus. *(Photograph © Michael H. Francis)*
Inset: Historically, scientists have recognized many geographic races of wolves, including twenty-four in North America. Today, scientists recognize only five geographic races of wolves. (Photograph © Michael H. Francis)

Figure 6

Figure 6: Geographic distribution of wolf subspecies recognized in North America:
1. Arctic wolf
2. Mexican wolf
3. Eastern timber wolf
4. Great Plains wolf
5. Northwestern wolf
(Data: U.S. Fish and Wildlife Service)

that, there clearly were too many wolf races recognized.

Enter Ron Nowak, a highly experienced wolf taxonomist. With the help of the U.S. Fish and Wildlife Service, he re-examined the wolf specimens from North America and revised the traditional classification in 1995. He used a combination of ten skull measurements and a computerized statistical method to segregate wolf skulls according to different areas of the wolf's range. His critical look reduced the total number of recognized subspecies in North America from twenty-four to five (Figure 6). Most wolf biologists welcomed this new classification system as being far more logical and biologically sound.

In this new classification, Minnesota wolves are no longer considered eastern timber wolves but rather are Great Plains wolves; this race once ranged from eastern Michigan across the United States to the California coast. (The actual range of the eastern timber wolf, according to Nowak, was the eastern United States and southeastern Canada; that race now remains only in southeastern Canada.)

Another way of classifying wolves, which has little direct connection to subspecies, involves different genetic strains of wolves. This system is based on DNA analysis but involves the use of a special kind of DNA called "mitochondrial DNA" (mtDNA). MtDNA happens to be an excellent marker of genetic strains. Twelve types of mtDNA have been recognized in North American wolves, and four of them are found in Minnesota.

Two of the Minnesota wolves' mtDNA types are the same as those found in coyotes in Minnesota and surroundings, which could mean that such wolves resulted from coyotes mating with wolves long ago. However, there are also other interpretations, so judgement about this question is still open. What is known so far indicates that at least one of Minnesota's strains ranges as far away as Alaska and another into Canada's Northwest Territories. Until more complete studies are done on the mtDNA types of wolves across more areas of North America, the full distribution of each of Minnesota's types cannot be known.

Appearance and Behavior

None of the methods of classification tell anything about the wolf's appearance or behavior. Minnesota wolves are about like any other wolf. They are a bit smaller than the Alaskan and northern Canadian

Most wolves in Minnesota are a mottled gray, but 1 to 3 percent may be black, and a very few even white. The presence of black or white wolves probably represents the influence of dispersing wolves from populations farther north, in Canada. There, the incidence of these color phases is much greater. (Photograph © D. R. Fernandez & M. L. Peck)

wolves and somewhat larger than their counterparts in southeastern Canada and the wolves to the south, such as the Mexican wolf and those of southern Eurasia.

Adult male Minnesota wolves range from 70 to 110 pounds (32 to 50 kg) and females from 40 to 90 pounds (18 to 41 kg). The animals stand up to 33 inches (84 cm) tall at the shoulders. Thus, they are two to three times the size of their cousins, the coyotes. Nevertheless, unless a person gets a good view, it can be hard to distinguish a wolf from a coyote.

Most Minnesota wolves are a typical mottled gray like most of the wolves throughout the world. However, about 1 percent of them are black, sometimes with a small white mark on their chest. An even smaller percentage of Minnesota wolves are white. I once studied a pack that lived along the Minnesota-Canada border and comprised three gray, one black, and one white wolf. Steve Fritts studied a radioed

white wolf in northwestern Minnesota and recorded three more during his aerial tracking there.

As some wolves get older, their fur begins to take on a frosty appearance and turn white. The Quadga Lake pack about fifteen miles (24 km) east-southeast of Ely during the 1970s was composed of a few such wolves, making me think the frosting effect had a genetic basis. This theory was borne out by two captive wolves I once obtained from the Chicago Zoo, a female about ten years old that had well-frosted fur and her two-year-old male offspring. When the male turned five years old, his fur began frosting as well.

It is interesting that the black color phase in Minnesota wolves is more prevalent the northeast corner of the state, east of Grand Rapids. Black wolves have also turned up in Wisconsin and Isle Royale, both areas east of Minnesota.

The eyes of Minnesota wolves generally are brown, but I have seen wolves whose eyes were yellow and even one whose eyes were blue. The latter animal was

Above: The eyes of most Minnesota wolves are brown, but others are yellow, and occasionally blue. Wolves can see well at night and during other periods of low light, which allows them to hunt at night. Wolves usually become active toward dusk and tend to rest a few hours after dawn. (Photograph © Erwin & Peggy Bauer)

Right: White wolves are very rare in Minnesota. A few were seen in both northeastern and northwestern Minnesota in the 1970s when the wolf population was first recovering. These animals probably represented dispersing wolves from Canada. Wolves inhabiting Canada's far north all are white, but some populations that are mostly white range as far south as within less than 1,000 miles of Minnesota. (Photograph © D. R. Fernandez & M. L. Peck)

a magnificent creature who sometimes weighed as much as 110 pounds (50 kg). I had a particularly good look at this animal one day with several other people when we captured it via a capture collar.

A capture collar is a special radio collar that some associates and I developed; it bears two anesthetic darts that sit just above the neck. When we want to examine a wolf wearing a capture collar, we home in on its radio signal, then send a special coded signal to the collar that fires one of the darts, and the animal is drugged.

One time when we were trying to so dart the blue-eyed wolf, we walked as close as we could to him and then sent the special signal. Suddenly the wolf barked from only about 100 feet (30 m) away as the dart injected. A few minutes later, the large, staggering wolf broke through the brush with his mate nudging him with her shoulder as though trying to hold him up. They came within a few yards of us when the mate saw us and ran off. Our wolf then flopped down just in front of us as the drug took full effect. He was a member of a newly formed pair that had not yet produced pups.

Packs

Most Minnesota wolf packs comprise a pair of wolves and some of their offspring from the last few years. A few packs I have seen, however, are less conventional. In one case, a breeding male whose mate had died remained with one of his male offspring over the offspring's first winter and then paired with a young female from a neighboring pack the following spring. For several months the trio operated as a pack. Another unconventional pack, which lived just east of Ely, was formed by a male that paired with two females (probably sisters) and bred them both.

A third type of unconventional pack in Minnesota is one composed of the standard family but with an extra member from some other pack. At least some evidence of this kind of pack composition has been found in northeastern, northwestern, and north-central Minnesota via radio-tracking. Genetic studies of Superior National Forest packs indicate that perhaps about one quarter of the packs have an outside member.

The typical pack of wolves, however, consists of a breeding pair, their pups, some yearlings from their previous litter, and sometimes offspring from the previous year or two. Usually by the time they are four years of age, all offspring have dispersed from

A capture collar is a special type of radio-collar that includes not only a standard signal transmitter but also a signal receiver, a computer, and two drug-filled darts poised above a wolf's neck. The collar was developed in Minnesota to allow biologists to, at any time, recapture a wolf that is wearing it. To do so, biologists send a special coded signal to the collar, which fires one of the darts. (The second dart is a back up.) Once the wolf's signal indicates that the wolf is drugged, biologists home in on the signal to find the wolf. (Photograph © Layne Kennedy)

Once a wolf is drugged by a capture collar, it lies there until biologists home in on it and find it. This usually takes twenty to thirty minutes, but the drug lasts at least forty-five minutes. The biologists can then re-weigh the wolf, take a new blood sample, and see how the wolf compares with its previous examination. (Photograph © L. David Mech)

Most Minnesota wolf packs consist of a pair of parent wolves and their surviving offspring from the previous two or three summers. By winter, even the pups born in spring are as large as their older brothers and sisters and their parents. Any pups that are unable to grow enough by winter usually die in fall. (Photograph © Michael H. Francis)

the pack. In a few cases an offspring will take over the breeding position from one of the parents. In the Perch Lake pack ten miles south of Ely, a three year old bred with her stepfather, two years after he had replaced her father, who apparently had been killed.

Minnesota wolf pack sizes vary from just two individuals (a mated pair) to as many as twenty-three. In northwestern, north-central, and east-central parts of Minnesota, the average winter pack size is about five or six, with a range from two to ten. The same is true for northeastern Minnesota except for the extreme northeast, where pack sizes tend to run larger. The main biological difference between extreme northeastern Minnesota and the rest of the state is that the wolf's major food in the former area is moose instead of deer.

Minnesota's largest wolf pack was discovered only recently—and far from the middle of the wilderness. John Stewart of Olgilvie, Minnesota, was bow hunting for deer between Hinckley and Highway 65 north of Mora during fall 1998. Perched in a tree stand, Stewart spotted a "wave of wolves" approaching.

"I started counting as accurately as I could under the circumstances. Three, seven, ten, to the front and sides; I turned—13, 17, 20!" he said. "As the main group moved on, three stragglers appeared." This unusual pack later sauntered up the driveway of nearby seasonal resident Shirley Kwapick some four and a half miles away, also in broad daylight.

Many people would say that prey size and pack size are related because it takes more wolves to kill larger prey. However, usually when wolves chase moose the wolves are strung out in line like a freight train; generally only the first few animals make the attack. It is true that once the attack proceeds, other members of the pack join in. How effective they are, however, remains unclear.

In any case, there are good records of single wolves killing adult moose, and considerable data shows that the larger the pack, the less food each wolf gets. This fact contradicts the idea that larger packs exist to kill larger prey.

Then why do larger packs live where there is larger prey?

First of all, that generalization itself is not tight. For instance, the pack of twenty-three wolves that John Stewart saw lived far south of the moose range, where the main prey is deer.

The average Minnesota wolf pack in winter contains five or six members. When times are hard for wolves, their pack sizes diminish, sometimes to the basic pair of parents. During better times, more offspring may remain with the pack longer, so pack sizes increase. The largest well-documented pack in Minnesota was seen northwest of Hinckley in fall 1998 and contained twenty-three wolves. (Photograph © Layne Kennedy)

The current thought is that wolves live in packs in order to allow them to help feed growing offspring, since the prey they kill are large enough to provide such food. If packs were smaller, they would have to spend more time keeping scavengers off kills or would waste more food. This also means, however, that when food is short, pack members may squabble, threatening each other in order to compete for what food is available. (Photograph © Karen Hollett)

Second, it might just be that instead of larger packs being needed to kill large prey, the relationship might work the other way—larger prey allow wolf packs to be larger. When a pair of wolves kills a large animal, there is usually far more food than they need at the time. With a 800- to 1,000-pound (363- to 454-kg) moose, much meat is left over. In winter, the extra meat will keep, but it is often eaten by other animals such as foxes, coyotes, ravens, and eagles. In summer, of course, carcasses decay within a few days, and all the surplus meat is lost. Wolves do cache a great deal of their prey, and that no doubt helps keep some of the meat from spoiling.

In any case, one way to take advantage of all the available meat at a kill is for the wolves to bring their offspring with them. According to well-accepted biological principle, all animal activity and behavior is ultimately dedicated to the individual's own survival and passing on his/her genes. The best way to pass on genes is to produce and nurture a large number of offspring.

By allowing offspring to accompany them during hunts, the breeding pair of wolves not only provides models for their offspring, but they also furnish their offspring with the surplus food. The larger the prey, the more offspring the breeding pair can bring with them. I have watched as many as fifteen wolves feed around a large moose carcass, but a deer supports only six or eight feeding wolves at a time.

Whatever explains the dynamics of wolf pack size, Minnesota's wolves are surely obeying some kind of ancient imperative that has forever served them well. It is comforting to know that because of the wolf population's dramatic recovery and the persistence still of Minnesota's wilderness, the wolf can now continue to obey those same laws far into the future.

Facing page: Rarely do pack members fight seriously. Although they snarl, growl, and sometimes even wrestle as they compete for a scarce food item, pack members spend most of their time in friendly activities and peaceful interactions. (Photograph © D. Robert Franz)

CHAPTER 5

Wolf Movements and Spacing in Minnesota
by Fred H. Harrington,
Roger P. Peters, and Russell J. Rothman

After searching for several hours, we found the radio signals of the Jackpine wolf pack at a site three miles (5 km) beyond the previous day's location. That site, near a small pond thirty miles (48 km) south of Ely, was just outside their territory and within that of the neighboring Harris Lake pack. Meanwhile, signals showed that the Harris Lake pack was less than two miles (3 km) away. What was behind this trespass? Why had the pups been led there? And what would result from this close encounter between two packs?

The first two questions had a simple answer: a dead moose. To answer the last question, we spent the next several days and nights at the site listening. Several times the packs howled back and forth, and the Harris Lake pack shifted from northwest to southwest of the Jackpine pack but maintained the same distance between the two packs. In three days, the Jackpine pack finished the moose and departed, leaving its pups to return two nights later to their territory.

This scenario illustrates several features of wolf movements. First, wolves travel to find food. Second, even ten- to fifteen-pound (5- to 7-kg) pups will travel long distances to eat. Third, wolves use a variety of signals to make their travels easier and safer. And finally, even pups can find their way around.

Facing page: Wolves travel an average of twelve to thirty miles a day and cover that distance at a steady, tireless five miles per hour. Whether crossing streams, rivers, or swamps or traveling on game trails, roadways, or ridges, wolves are superbly built for making their way over the terrain. Their large feet are not only blocky for good running, but they are highly flexible for excellent gripping of rough surfaces. (Photograph © Michael Francis)
Inset: Much of what has been learned in the past three decades about wolf movements and spacing was first discovered in Minnesota. From the sizes and extent of wolf pack territories to the exceedingly long distances that young wolves disperse—and much information in between—the intensive and extensive application of aerial radio-tracking of wolves has yielded a bonanza of information. (Photograph © L. David Mech)

Wolves probably know at all times where they are in relation to their territory boundary, when they have stepped outside of their area, and which way to go to return. Experimentally translocated wolves find their way back from distances as far as forty miles from their territories. (Photograph © D. R. Fernandez & M. L. Peck)

"The wolf is fed by his feet" is a Russian saying that aptly characterizes the importance of space for a wolf. Wolves prey primarily on large hoofed animals like deer and moose, which live in low numbers unevenly in the forest. Vulnerable prey, such as old deer or sick moose, are even rarer (see chapter 7). Thus, wolves must search and search before they find the right prey to kill.

While hunting, wolves travel an average twelve to thirty miles (19 to 48 km) a day at a modest pace of about five miles (8 km) an hour. They get the best returns for their travel by staying in familiar country. There they learn where prey can be found and can concentrate in the right areas. In addition, by remaining within its own area, a pack is less likely to encounter other packs. By defending its area, a pack can limit competition for prey and provide a safer environment for pups.

Territories

Wolf packs and pairs are territorial. A pack's territory must be large enough to provide enough vulnerable prey, and the density and seasonal availability of that prey are important.

The maximum territory size is set partly by prey density: the higher the prey density, the smaller the territory. Neighboring packs, however, are the greatest influence on maximum territory size. In an area of northwestern Minnesota being colonized by wolves during the 1970s, territories were relatively large, ranging from 75 to 215 square miles (194 to 557 square km), as packs were free to use as much space as they wanted. During the same period in northeastern Minnesota, on the other hand, territories were smaller, reduced by the presence of neighbors.

Territories near the Lake Superior shore deeryard cover only 20 to 50 square miles (52 to 130 square

Figure 7

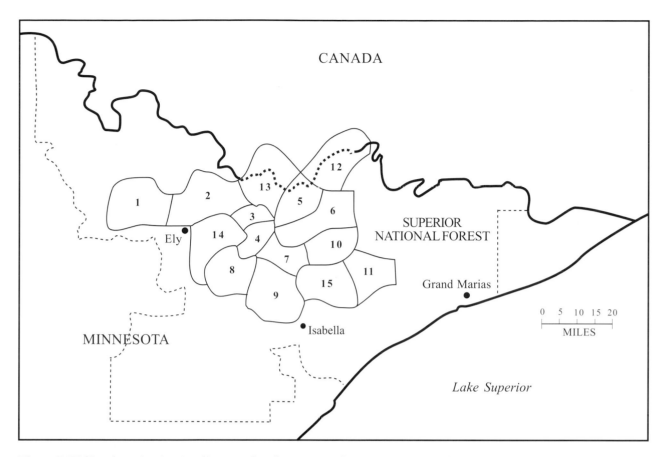

Figure 7: Wolf pack territories of radio-tagged packs in part of the Superior National Forest. Similar territories exist throughout the wolf range. (Data: L. David Mech, Biological Resources Division, U.S. Geological Survey)

km). Within central Superior National Forest, deer densities are lower and some regions are devoid of deer during winter. Consequently, wolf pack territories there range from 50 to 120 square miles (130 to 311 square km). In north-central Minnesota, Researcher Todd Fuller found that territories vary from 30 to 60 square miles (78 to 155 square km) in extent.

Territories provide sustenance for more than just the adult pair. Packs that raise pups often double in size from one year to the next. Thus, a territory needs to be large enough to support these extra wolves.

Wolf pack territories in an established population like that in northeastern Minnesota form a fairly stable mosaic (Figure 7). The greatest changes occur when a pack disappears because of failure to reproduce or because of lethal aggression from neighbors. When a territorial void occurs, the borders of adjacent pack territories realign, or a new pack establishes itself in the vacated area. Thus, most suitable habitat is usually claimed by one pack or another, with territories abutting each other.

Communication: Howling and Scent-marking

Packs maintain their territorial claims by howling and scent-marking, using these two behaviors in complementary ways. Howling provides an immediate means for packs to advertise over great distances, at times as far as six miles (10 km). Thus, a pack howl could cover an area of up to thirty square miles (78 square km), a sizable part of a Minnesota pack's territory. However, such howls operate less like bird songs, covering an entire territory, and more like a train whistle, warning when the pack is in the general vicinity.

It is easy for other wolves to pinpoint a pack's chorus howl. We often had wolves come up to us when we howled to them as part of our studies. It is quite a thrill in the dark of night to hear the brush around you crackle as a wolf approaches. It may be hard for wolves to judge the size of the pack from their howls, however. A chorus may exaggerate a pack's size, so other wolves may be reluctant to approach—seeking out a larger pack could be fatal. Thus, packs usually howl to avoid each other, which is most important when they are near their borders, eating prey, or occupying a rendezvous site. In the latter situations, howling helps protect important resources.

Howling may not reach more distant parts of a territory, and on stormy or windy nights, choruses may not carry more than a few hundred yards. Thus, howling has limitations for territory maintenance. Scent-marking, however, provides a complementary means of territory advertisement that overcomes some of these limitations. It gives wolves a widespread and long-lasting way of advertising, despite the relatively short range over which wolves can detect scent-marks.

Raised-leg urination (RLU) is the most important form of wolf scent-marking. RLUs are directed at conspicuous targets, such as trees, shrubs, rocks, and snowbanks. There they become hard to miss. RLUs release urine's pungent odor by increasing its evaporating surface as it trickles downward, letting wind waft it widely, and keeping it from being covered by snow or washed away by rain.

In addition to RLUs, defecations (scats) also serve as scent-marks. They are often deposited on prominent objects, such as snowbanks, stumps, and, in one case, an empty Hamm's beer can. After an RLU or defecation, wolves often scratch nearby, pawing the ground with vigorous alternate motions of the stiffened forelegs and opposite-side rear leg. Scratching creates a visual signal, and glands between the toes may add odor.

Only mature, dominant wolves—both male and female—leave RLUs, often along with snarling, growling, biting, or other displays of aggression or dominance. Wolves squirt about one RLU per 500 yards (457 m), and they regularly re-mark, even when no other wolves have visited. A pack's own RLUs are the most common stimuli for re-marking.

When pack members howl as a group, the chorus howl helps advertise their presence to nearby neighboring packs. Those packs sometimes reply, and each then knows where the other is and knows what area to avoid so as to minimize fighting. (Photograph © Karen Hollett)

Raised-leg urination (RLU) is an important form of scent-marking familiar to almost anyone with a dog. In wolves, it is almost exclusively the breeding male and female that raise-leg urinate, and they do so year-round. However, their highest rate of raised-leg urination takes place around the breeding season. (Photograph © Karen Hollett)

Facing page: Howling helps wolves stay in contact with their packmates. When separated, for example after chasing a prey animal far and wide, wolves learn where each other is, and the pack can then re-assemble before continuing on their travels. (Photograph © D. Robert Franz)

Figure 8

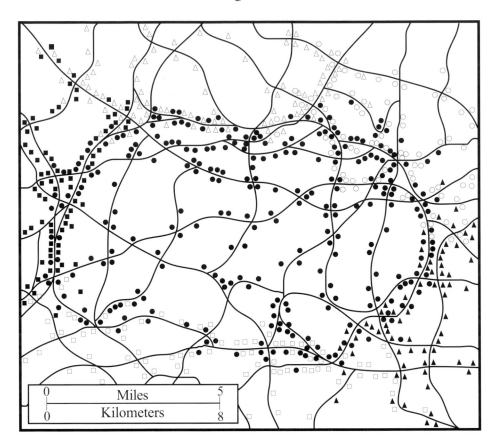

Figure 8: Hypothetical map of wolf scent-mark distribution in a wolf pack territory. Approximate frequency and distribution are based on actual data, assuming wolf trails are as shown. Different symbols represent the scent marks of different packs. (Data: L. David Mech, Biological Resources Division, U.S. Geological Survey)

Urine marks made by wolves urinating with raised leg are quite apparent in the snow, for they are usually left on rocks, snowbanks, small shrubs, beer cans, and other conspicuous objects. Wolves leave such RLUs about every 500 yards (457 m) on average, and during winter they may be detectable by other wolves for two weeks or more. (Photograph © Bill Marchel)

RLUs last at least a week or two; Roger's Samoyed dog Freyja often sniffed at wolf RLUs at least two weeks old, and in winter Russ often could both see and smell them when they were a month old. The number of RLUs increases throughout winter from about two and a half per 1,000 yards (914 m) in December and January to three and a half per 1,000 yards in the late-February breeding season, and then dropping to about one per 1,000 yards in March. The number of squat urinations (SQUs) produced by subordinate females also peaks in late February, suggesting that SQUs are also related to breeding.

When wolves find fresh signs of a neighboring pack, they abruptly increase their RLU rate. The rate of RLUs at the edges of territories, where wolves find signs of other packs, is more than twice that in the centers. These high rates of marking concentrate marks along territory borders, where both packs mark and stimulate marking by each other (Figure 8).

A one-to-two-mile-wide (1.6-to-3.2-km) area

Wolves travel on a network of logging roads, deer and moose trails, ridges, beaver dams, and other easy routes. Because the animals travel up to thirty miles a day searching for prey they can catch, any efficiency they can practice helps further their lives. (Photograph © L. David Mech)

around a pack's territory forms a "buffer" zone. Packs tend to scent-mark at high rates there, but they also use these zones least, reflecting a fear of neighbors. In both northeastern and northwestern Minnesota wolves kill fewer deer in these buffer zones than in the centers of their territories.

Pack Behavior and Dispersal

Strife between packs is the most frequent cause of death for adult wolves in the wild. Packs fight most often within the buffer zones or outside their territory. Although many wolf deaths may result from packs accidentally meeting, packs also sometimes deliberately stalk their neighbors.

Most often, however, packs simply avoid each other. Thus, the outcome of an encounter depends on a number of factors, including whether or not the wolves can actually see each other. If they can, they can easily assess each other's size; then the larger pack usually chases the smaller. Without visual con-

tact, however, the uncertainty probably helps lead to avoidance.

For example, the Birch Lake pack once chased and mortally wounded a deer within the buffer area shared with the Harris Lake pack. The deer ran south into the Harris Lake pack's territory, but, though there was no visible sign of the Harris Lake pack, the Birch Lake pack did not follow. Instead, they scent-marked heavily and then returned to their territory. The deer lay dead only about fifty feet (15 m) from where the pack turned back—a powerful testimony to the trespassing pack's aversion to their neighbors.

Wolves travel on a complex network of game paths, old logging trails, dirt roads, and other established routes. During snow-free periods, they cover up to thirty miles (48 km) each day. In winter, even though snow impedes them, they can still travel similar distances, because they use frozen waterways or windblown ridges and travel single file.

A pack uses its territory irregularly but reaches

Most dispersing wolves leave their natal packs as lone wolves (like this wild wolf crossing a prairie) and travel long distances away from their pack's territory. Often such wolves make one to five "trial" runs, leaving the pack and heading forty miles or so away and then returning after a few weeks or months. Are they exploring new areas? Gauging what other wolves are out there? Looking for possible mates? No one knows for sure yet. (Photograph © Bill Marchel)

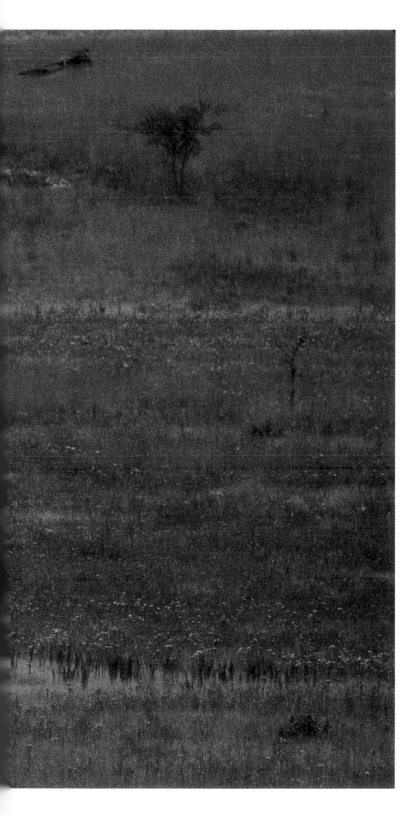

most of it at least every three weeks. In winter, the wolves encounter and leave a RLU, scat, or SQU about every 240 yards (219 m). RLUs are densest in frequently visited places, especially trail junctions. Thus, the entire territory is studded with odor "hotspots," so that any traveling wolf soon detects a mark. These olfactory markers form part of the well-organized memories or "cognitive maps" that wolves possess to help them find their way and recognize territorial edges.

Each year, as a pack expands with more pups, pressure increases on existing members to seek new opportunities elsewhere. Wolves of both sexes leave the pack. Yearlings are the age-class most likely to leave. Maturation, food competition, and social status are likely the primary influences on dispersal. Yearlings or adults of low rank may disperse from the pack rather than bide their time in hopes of one day breeding within their natal territory.

Many dispersers make at least one foray outside their territory before leaving altogether. These "test-runs," lasting anywhere from two days to months, may give a wolf some idea as to what opportunities exist beyond its territory. Once they finally leave, most dispersers travel alone and maintain a low profile.

How far a wolf goes from its original pack depends on several factors. It may simply travel around the edges of its territory, perhaps as little as a mile or two, or it may travel more than 500 miles (805 km) away.

Wolves display two types of long-distance dispersal: nomadism and directional dispersal. Nomadism enables a loner to repeatedly search a relatively restricted area for any new living opportunities. If a suitable area becomes vacant, the nomad may discover it quickly. However, individuals can wander for years and travel a great distance while seeking out a suitable vacancy and a mate. Although nomadism works for some wolves, many nomads die from accidents or encounters with territorial packs before they find a suitable opening in another territory.

The other option for a disperser is directional dispersal, or sustained movement in a single direction. One Minnesota disperser that Steve Fritts tagged traveled a straight-line distance of 530 miles (853 km) between its capture site south of International Falls and eastern Saskatchewan where it was killed. Others have moved several hundred miles, ending

Figure 9

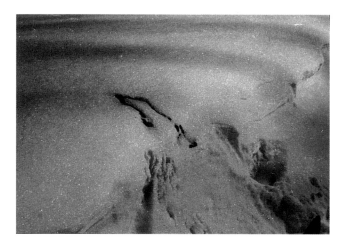

Figure 9: Dispersal route of a satellite-collared female wolf from Camp Ripley in central Minnesota, February 5 to July 22, 1999. (Data: L. David Mech, Biological Resources Division, U.S. Geological Survey and S. B. Merrill, Minnesota Department of Natural Resources)

One of the most significant types of wolf scent-marking is the double raised-leg urination, performed by the pack's breeding male and breeding female. Each time one member of the mated pair urinates with raised leg, the other member marks similarly, within a few inches. When close to the breeding season, the female mark contains vaginal blood, a sign that she is approaching heat, or estrus. This double mark tells other wolves that the wolves holding the territory are mated. (Photograph © L. David Mech)

up in Wisconsin or Michigan. The likely function of such sustained travel may be to quickly move to the frontier of the population, where suitable vacant range may be more easily found.

The return of wolves to Michigan and Wisconsin no doubt resulted from long-distance dispersers from Minnesota; some wolves traveled well over 120 miles (193 km) eastward to Wisconsin and Michigan, where they paired and settled. Others dispersed to North and South Dakota where they were illegally or accidentally killed. During their travels, they had to have overcome many obstacles, such as rivers, lakes, busy interstate highways, and even residential areas in rural and urban regions (see Figure 9).

Lone wolves maintain a low profile when cutting through wolf country, rarely scent-marking or replying to howls. They do, however, investigate resident pack scent-marks and the howling of single wolves with what appears to be great interest. One lone wolf dug out more than two cubic feet (0.06 cubic m) of snow to uncover what was likely a resident wolf's scent-mark, and it similarly dug out several others. One female traveled more than thirteen miles (21 km) away in a day after detecting a nearby pack's presence. Lone wolves never replied to simulated howling, but several times during the breeding season, they approached the howler closely and quietly.

New Pairs and Packs

It seems clear then how "reading" scent-marks and howling can direct and funnel dispersers into unoccupied areas where the chance of finding a potential mate would be enhanced. However, once two wolves of the opposite sex meet in a potential territory, a successful pairing is not guaranteed any more than it might be in humans. Lone wolves sometimes associate for several days, then break up and disperse separately.

Newly formed pairs probably stay together because they established a physical and behavioral synchrony during courtship. This synchrony may be stimulated when they scent-mark together or double mark. Double marking occurs when one animal urinates, using a raised leg, followed by the mate's immediate investigation of the mark and then its own RLU. Established pairs double mark at their highest rates during the breeding season, indicating the importance of double marking in courtship and breed-

Lone, dispersing wolves keep a low profile while traveling through other wolf pack territories. They rarely scent mark or reply to howls, for if detected, they may be killed. One lone wolf traveled more than thirteen miles immediately after detecting a nearby pack's presence. (Photograph © Lynn M. Stone)

ing. Russ found that new pairs double-mark at the highest rate of all and do a great deal of mutual sniffing of each other's marks. He explained this behavior succinctly: "Wolves that pee together stay together."

Scent-marks probably also show whether a mated pair exists in a pack, or whether there is an opportunity for a loner to integrate into the pack as one of the breeders. Thus, a "studious" reading of scent-marks and howling reduces chances of hostile encounters while increasing the chance of finding a potential mate. Once two loners of opposite sex meet and pair, their scent-marks quickly cement their claim to a territory, and their howling duets may further solidify their claim.

When a pair of wolves howls in chorus, human observers regularly overestimate the size of the group. We typically "heard" four to five wolves rather than the pair actually doing the howling. This multiplying effect likely fools wolves as well, allowing newly formed pairs to better compete for a territory. Thus, lone wolves quickly fill any voids in a population's territorial mosaic. They also provide continual pressure for expansion at the edges of the population's range.

With the wolf's high reproductive rate (see chapter 6), long dispersal abilities, and complex signaling systems, it is easy to see how the species so readily re-established itself across northern Minnesota.

CHAPTER 6

Wolf Numbers and Reproduction
by L. David Mech

Reproduction in wolves is a prolonged process. In many animals we think of reproduction as merely the production of young. The life history of wolves, however, is also characterized by a relatively long dependence and apprenticeship by the offspring until they themselves are ready to go off and reproduce. In fact, these features are the basis of the wolf-pack structure—a pair of parents and their offspring.

Age of first reproduction in Minnesota wolves varies a great deal, just as it does elsewhere. In captivity, both male and female wolves have produced young at one year of age. This early reproduction has not been observed in the wild. However, two-year-old wolves, both male and female, have bred both in central and northwestern Minnesota. Nevertheless, in the saturated wolf population of northeastern Minnesota, females do not usually breed until they are at least three years old, and I have found one animal this age that still had not reproductively matured. From a hormonal standpoint, wolves may not be fully mature—say comparable to a twenty-five-year-old human—until about five years old.

The Mating Game

Reproductively ready wolves can meet eligible mates in several ways, and Minnesota wolves use all of them. Science does not yet know enough about what an eligible mate is except that, unless there is no alternative, the mate cannot be closely related, such as a parent, offspring,

Facing page: Pups form the center of attraction for members of wolf packs, for the pack is a family whose main function is the production and nurturing of offspring, similar to that of a human family. Some anthropologists believe that the wolf pack is a better model for a human family than are the groups of other primates such as chimpanzees and gorillas. (Photograph © Erwin & Peggy Bauer)

Inset: Wolves are about as monogamous as people. Generally, mated pairs stay together for several years. But if one dies, the other may take a new mate, or even if both survive, one may switch mates. In some cases, males have bred with two females. Most often, however, packs contain a single mated pair of parents. (Photograph © Alan & Sandy Carey)

Above: Most wolf pairs form when dispersed members of different packs meet up, get along, and pair bond. They may remain together for a year or so before producing pups, or they may produce them during their first breeding season. This timing probably depends on their ages. (Photograph © D. Robert Franz)

Right: During the breeding season, mature female wolves tend to travel with their mate half a length behind. This not only allows the breeding male to guard against another male's attempt at copulation with his mate, but it also means he can remain instantly available when the female's condition beckons. Receptive females avert their tails. When about to copulate, individual mated pairs often move out of the main pack for a few days, probably to avoid interference from other pack members. Sometimes pack associates try to get in on the mating, or they harass the mated pair while they are stuck together during copulation. (Photograph © Karen Hollett)

or sibling. Finding a genetically suitable mate, of course, is of utmost importance. Sometimes it is as simple as courting a neighbor. In an unusual example of this simple process, two maturing males of the Perch Lake pack south of Ely, in two consecutive years, each paired with the same mature female from the adjacent Birch Lake pack whose mate had left. The first male was killed illegally after pairing, and his younger brother then stepped in.

A second approach is for wolves to breed with a step-parent in the same pack. I saw such a pairing in 1976 when female Wolf 5176 apparently ousted her mother, Wolf 2473, and then mated with her mother's partner, which had replaced Wolf 5176's father. This new pair continued to produce pups for the next nine years until Wolf 5176 was killed by other wolves.

The remaining methods of pair bonding all involve dispersal from a pack and circulation about the population. Sometimes such a "floating" wolf can merely find a pack that has lost a breeder of the same sex and replace it, as happened in the Perch Lake pack.

In northwestern Minnesota, graduate student Steve Fritts saw another approach. Some wolves would disperse, meet a mate doing the same thing, and then float as a pair until they found a place to squeeze in among the existing territories. Then they started their own territory and pack. However, I have never seen this approach used any other place. Floaters tend to frequent certain areas among the pack territories, meet a mate at one of these places, and occupy that area. In Fritts's study, most dispersers paired within a few days of leaving their packs, whereas in the saturated wolf population in the Superior National Forest, it sometimes took loners as much as a year to find a mate.

In still other cases, dispersers travel long distances, and through the process described in chapter 5, find a mate and settle. These are the types of dispersers that can expand the wolf's range and colonize new areas.

Bonding and Breeding

Wolves have long been considered monogamous. However, in reality, wolves are about as monogamous—or non-monogamous—as human beings. In the Perch Lake pack, Wolf 5176 and Wolf 5132 ap-

parently mated only with each other for a nine-year period, a strong record of monogamy. However, as indicated above, Wolf 5132 had also mated with Wolf 5176's mother for two years before. This approach is called serial monogamy, a trait well known in humans.

While monogamy or serial monogamy may well be the rule in Minnesota wolves, I have also seen polygyny. In 1987, male Wolf 6895 was seen throughout the courtship and mating season with both female Wolf 1831 and female Wolf 6767 a few miles east of Ely. The three animals traveled as a trio for the next few months until April 3 when the females parted and denned fifteen miles (24 km) apart. Both produced pups and raised them. Male 6895 spent most of his time with female 1831, although at least on one occasion he visited female 6767 at her den.

I have not observed any female wolf in Minnesota either bonding or copulating with more than one male during a given breeding season, nor do I know of any such records in wild wolves. Such an observation would be difficult to make, however, so any evidence of multiple paternity will probably have to be documented by genetic studies that show siblings sired by different mates.

Females do not have to be sexually mature to bond with males. One radioed female that dispersed from a pack at seventeen months of age paired at nineteen months and set up a territory. Then, during the first month of denning season, the pair localized in an area of about one square mile (2.6 square km). They then split, and the female returned to her natal pack. There she remained for the next six months. When she died at the age of thirty-four months, an autopsy revealed she had not yet sexually matured.

When lone wolves of opposite sex meet, they begin double scent-marking as detailed in chapter 5. This process solidifies their pair bonding and can be done any time of year.

Northern Minnesota wolves may breed any time between about January 28 and March 4. As the breeding season approaches, the members of a mated pair sleep closer and closer together. During the breeding season, mature females tend to travel at the head of the pack with their mate half a length behind. Not only does this allow the breeding male to guard against another male's attempt at copulation with

Above: Wolf dens are often rock caves, holes in sandy ground that may be enlarged fox or coyote dens, hollow logs, old beaver lodges, or merely depressions in the top of the ground. Sometimes wolves bear their pups under the low overhanging boughs of thick conifers. Even though wolves only use dens in spring, they may prepare these dens as early as fall, and they sometimes keep several dens ready, probably as insurance in case one caves in, floods, or otherwise becomes unusable. Dens are used only for the first eight weeks of the pups' lives. Contrary to popular belief, wolves do not live in dens year-round. Some dens, especially natal dens above ground, are abandoned after only three or four weeks. (Photograph © Lynn & Donna Rogers)

Right: If a mother wolf needs to move a pup, she grasps it gently in her mouth and carries it. This is necessary when pups are too small to follow their mother on their own. In Alaska, one wolf carried her pups one-by-one about ten miles from one den to another. Usually the mother wolf is the only pack member that will carry a pup. (Photograph © Lynn & Donna Rogers)

his mate, but it also means he can remain instantly available when the female's condition beckons.

Receptive females avert their tail. When about to copulate, individual mated pairs often move out of the main pack for a few days, probably to avoid interference from other pack members. Sometimes pack associates try to get in on the mating, or they harass the mated pair while they are stuck together during copulation.

Wolves copulate like dogs, the male mounting the female from behind. The male inserts his penis, and the base of his penis swells; the female's vaginal sphincter muscle locks around it, tying the pair together. While tied, the male dismounts, swivels around, and the two animals then "hang up" tail-to-tail the same way as dogs do when mating, for up to thirty minutes. During this time the male ejaculates frequently. No one knows exactly why the copulatory tie occurs. However, it may help to ensure passage of sperm to the eggs and make certain no competitor sneaks in on the act.

The Life of Pups

The gestation period for wolves is sixty-two to sixty-three days. Thus, pups are usually born from about early April to early May in northern Minnesota. The average litter size is six pups, and almost every pack produces a litter each year. Newly formed pairs do not necessarily bear pups in their first year.

Depending upon the sites available, dens are often rock caves, holes in the sandy ground that may be enlarged fox or coyote dens, hollow logs, old beaver lodges, or merely depressions in the top of the ground. Sometimes wolves bear their pups under the low overhanging boughs of thick conifers.

Newborn wolf pups are quite hardy. Even within 600 miles (966 km) of the North Pole, I have seen pups in ground depressions survive light rain and snow when only ten days old. Although their mother usually remains with the pups during their first three weeks of age, she must sometimes leave them, at least to drink water. (Her mate and other pack members deliver food to her.) I knew of one mother in the High Arctic that left her ten-to-fifteen-day-old pups alone in a ground depression for over two hours.

Dens are used only for the first eight weeks of the pups' lives. Contrary to popular belief, wolves do not live in dens year-round. Some dens, especially

To sleep, wolf pups often huddle together in a pile for warmth, sometimes even as late as in September. By then they are living in a rendezvous site, or "loafing area," above ground, which may be far from the den. There they also romp and play, and wait for the adult members to return and bring them food. (Photograph © Lynn & Donna Rogers)

Newborn wolf pups are quite hardy. Even pups in ground depressions survive light rain and snow when only ten days old. Although their mother usually remains with the pups during their first three weeks of life, she must sometimes leave them, at least to drink water. (Her mate and other pack members deliver food to her.) This four-to-five-week-old pup is already exploring the area around its den. (Photograph © Lynn & Donna Rogers)

Wolf pups grow and develop quickly, gaining an average of about 1.3 pounds (0.6 kg) each week when 14 to 27 weeks old. As the animals develop, their puppy ears and nose elongate, their adult guard hairs appear and the pups begin looking like adults by November. They may reach 70 pounds (32 kg) by this time. (Top: Photograph © Fred H. Harrington; Middle: Photograph © Erwin & Peggy Bauer; Bottom: Photograph © Lynn & Donna Rogers)

natal dens above ground, are abandoned after only three or four weeks, with the pups being moved to another den. In any case, after about eight weeks, wolves move their pups to an area known as a rendezvous site. Fritts found in northwestern Minnesota that the distance between the den and the first rendezvous site varied from one and a half to six miles (2 to 10 km).

A rendezvous site is a nest on the ground where the pups huddle together when sleeping, and thus it is where all the pack members rendezvous. Such sites may be right around the natal den or miles from it. Sometimes a single site is used all summer, whereas in other cases wolves shift sites every few weeks. Sometimes wolves establish a rendezvous site where they kill a large prey animal. Then they merely lead the pups to the carcass rather than continue to carry food from the carcass to the pups.

Known as "loafing areas" by earlier writers, rendezvous sites are places where pups can hang out and rest while the adults expend energy searching for food and bringing it to them. Such a system maximizes pup growth so that by winter the pups would be large enough to follow the adults on the hunt, usually starting in October.

Well-fed, healthy Minnesota wolf pups can attain as much as seventy pounds (32 kg) by their first November. Essentially, they become adult sized by then. Their milk canine teeth have been shed, and their permanent canines have grown most of their full length—about one inch (2.5 cm). (A second inch of canine root anchors these important teeth into their skull.)

Thus, when watching a pack of wolves during winter, it is often impossible to distinguish pups from other pack members merely by size, unless the pups are runty. Some of the runts will not make it through winter.

Wolf pups in Minnesota, and probably elsewhere, can survive on their own when only four or five months old. Radio-tagged pups of this age have survived even though experimentally separated from their parents and other pack mates and moved many miles from home.

Minnesota wolf pups almost always remain with their packs until at least ten months of age and usually longer. However, by about a year of age some 10

Pups nurse over a period of seven to nine weeks, although when three weeks old they also begin eating solid food regurgitated by adult pack members. Nursing bouts last one to four minutes every three to four hours. The pups keep their puppy canine teeth until about six months of age, when these "milk" teeth are replaced by adult fangs. (Photograph © Erwin & Peggy Bauer)

to 15 percent of these animals have left their natal packs and dispersed. Another 45 to 50 percent disperse over the following year, and the rest disperse when two to three years old.

Population Fluctuations and Wolf Mortality

Thus, a wolf pack can be seen as a reproducing system, complete with finishing school where its offspring apprentice on the hunt until time to leave and spread the pack's genes far and wide. As each pack annually churns out dispersers, these animals compete to use the area's prey resources, expand the population, and increase the species' range (see chapter 5). Some make it; some do not. Over a large area and a long period, the most fit tend to survive the best, produce the most offspring, and further the species' evolution.

When prey conditions are poor, fewer pups are

born and disperse, the population stagnates, at least temporarily, and the colonization of new areas is minimal. However, since wolves can live for more than a decade, the breeders continue to hold their territories and may compete with neighbors to expand. This tension results in more social strife and mortality, but the population survives at a lower density. A lower density helps allow recovery of the prey population, and eventually the system may thrive again.

A high density for Minnesota wolves is about one per ten square miles (26 square km). Currently, the Minnesota wolf population average density is about one wolf per twelve square miles (31 square km), according to calculations based on data from the Minnesota DNR.

A thriving wolf population can increase at a high rate. Because average pack size in Minnesota is five to

Each thriving wolf pack annually pumps out dispersing lone wolves that travel far and wide. These wolves carry their parents' genes to new areas. If the dispersers mate, they continue to pass on those genes in packs that compete with each other and help further the species' evolution. (Photograph © L. David Mech)

six wolves and average litter size is five to six pups, a wolf population can potentially double each year. All it takes is an adequate prey population and protection from humans. Each year, Minnesota's estimated 400 wolf packs produce more than 2,000 pups.

Thus, wolves colonizing new areas such as Wisconsin, Michigan, or central Minnesota have demonstrated high increases in population. Despite illegal and accidental human killing, natural mortality, and, in Minnesota, a government wolf-control program, the wolf population in these states has increased 5 to 40 percent each year for several years.

Where wolves are protected from human-caused mortality, more die from natural causes. Starvation of pups and death by other wolves are the usual means. In local areas, disease such as canine parvovirus, mange, and coccidiosis take a few wolves.

One wolf even died from blastomycosis, a fungus infecting the lungs. This wolf, when on its last legs, approached an isolated cabin and kept bumping against the window. "Stunned, we stared at the face pressed against the glass, at the blazing yellow eyes and broad cheek ruffs of an adult wolf," the inhabitants wrote. The people put a blanket around the wolf, brought it inside at 3:30 A.M., and tried to nurture it. The animal finally died a few hours later, the only wolf known to have died from the disease.

In thriving wolf populations, such natural mortality factors as those listed above are usually not enough to hold wolf numbers down. The result has been the continuing increase in the number of wolves and heartening wolf recovery we have seen in Wisconsin, Michigan, and Minnesota over the last two decades.

CHAPTER 7

Minnesota Wolf Predation
by L. David Mech

It looked like a pretty clear-cut contest—seven wolves versus a single deer. As I circled in an aircraft above this natural drama in the Superior National Forest, it appeared that the wolves would soon have their supper.

The fact that they did not formed the beginning of a long string of lessons I would learn in thirty years of studying wolf predation on deer. Even though deer are one of the smallest of the wolf's regular prey species, they are not necessarily easy to catch, even for a large pack of wolves.

As will be apparent in later chapters, deer possess many physical and behavioral traits that help them survive in the face of Minnesota's large wolf population. It is true that deer do make up the main prey of Minnesota's wolves. Probably some 95 percent of the state's wolves rely on deer. The rest, especially wolves in the northeastern part of the Boundary Waters Canoe Area Wilderness (BWCAW) where no deer live in winter, feed mostly on moose.

It is fair to say that wherever wolves live, in Minnesota or elsewhere, they feed on whatever large prey are available. This usually means hoofed mammals, but wolves will supplement their diet with anything they can catch: beavers, snowshoe hares, squirrels, mice, domestic sheep, goats, pigs, cows, horses, turkeys, and even dogs.

If wolves live in an area with some kind of prey animal, they will learn to exploit that species. For instance, in Yellowstone National Park, wolves that had never killed buffalo (bison)—their most formidable prey—learned to do so within a couple of years.

Facing page: Wolves prey on whatever large hoofed animals are available, such as deer, moose, elk, caribou, bison, musk-oxen, antelope, mountain sheep, and mountain goats. In Minnesota, both white-tailed deer and moose are the wolf's main prey, but statewide, deer form the majority of prey killed. (Photograph © Michael H. Francis)
Inset: Because most prey are alert and fleet, wolves must be able to run at least as fast. Some figures show that wolves can run thirty-five to forty miles (56 to 64 km) per hour. In addition, wolves must be able to run for long periods in order to outlast their prey. One wolf at least eleven years old was known to run at top speed for six to seven minutes. (Photograph © D. Robert Franz)

Above: Even though deer can run very fast, wolves sometimes catch them because some deer are less alert, slow, old, or otherwise weak. The trick for wolves is to find these individuals, and to do so, the wolves must attempt to catch any deer they encounter. Most of them get away, but sooner or later the wolves catch one. (Photograph © L. David Mech)

Right: Wolves can eat as much as twenty-two pounds of meat at a time, and they can eat more than one meal a day. They may then go hungry for days at a time. This feast-or-famine existence is necessary for animals that have to catch large prey, for it is not always possible to catch animals at just any time. However, when wolves do succeed, their prey is often large enough to let them gorge. On average, Minnesota wolves probably eat about five to six pounds per day. (Photograph © Michael H. Francis)

One of the main types of deer wolves kill are older ones, especially those over five years old. As any animal gets older, it eventually grows weaker and is less able to escape. Buck deer over five years old may start getting arthritis, or parasites can build up and further weaken older deer. (Photograph © Bill Marchel)

A fawn's spots help it blend into the forest floor where the animal hunkers down much of the time to avoid detection. There is also evidence that newborn fawns may not be detectable by odor. These and other traits help the fawn survive in wolf country. Nevertheless fawns are weaker and less experienced than older deer. Thus, wolves still tend to catch a large number of them. (Photograph © Bill Peterson)

Wolf vs. Whitetail

But how can wolves learn to kill buffalo and still have trouble catching deer? The short answer to this penetrating question is that whatever prey wolves are hunting they must find just the right individual or perhaps just the right situation: a prey animal at some disadvantage. A simple example would be an old moose on its last legs, starving to death from a harsh winter and perhaps studded with thousands of blood-sucking ticks. Even a single wolf could bring down such a stricken beast.

Amplify that example with every conceivable variation. The result explains the single most puzzling dilemma people face in trying to understand how wolves and their prey can live together forever— prey animals must be well enough adapted to survive long enough to reproduce and keep their population going; wolves must be well enough adapted to overcome prey adaptations often enough to catch and kill enough to eat, reproduce, and maintain their own populations.

How much does this amount to? That depends on the situation. Minnesota wolves can eat twenty-two pounds (10 kg) in one meal, and if food is plentiful, they may eat more than one meal per day. However, with their feast-or-famine lifestyle, they often go days without eating.

An average of about five and a half pounds (2.5 kg) of food per day will support a Minnesota wolf and allow it to reproduce. This average amount of food would require each wolf to kill the equivalent of fifteen to twenty adult-sized deer each year, depending on the amount of other prey they eat.

In the wolf-deer system, Minnesota wolves are able to find, catch, and kill enough deer through seeking out individuals of any of the following varieties:

1. older individuals, which presumably are less alert, slower, and weaker;
2. deer with injuries, such as broken legs and arthritic hooves;
3. deer weak from poor nutritional condition, because of hard winters, deep snow, and cold that make it hard for deer to get enough food;
4. deer less than a year old (fawns), which generally are weaker and less experienced at eluding predators;
5. newborn fawns that are underweight;
6. deer whose mothers or grandmothers were poorly nourished while pregnant;
7. bucks during and after the fall mating season (the rut) when they weaken themselves by fighting, fasting, and chasing does;
8. deer migrating between summer ranges and winter range (the reason for their vulnerability at this time remains unknown).

Although it is obvious in many of the above cases why wolves can more easily kill those types of deer,

Moose form the main diet of wolves in the few places in the Minnesota wolf range where deer are absent, such as the east-central part of the Boundary Waters Canoe Area Wilderness. Although moose are much larger than deer, wolves are still able to kill moose by finding old, sick, young, and weak individuals. Of course, when wolves do kill an 800- to 1,000-pound (363- to 454-kg) moose, they have enough food for a long time. On the other hand, it probably is much riskier for wolves to kill moose because even weak moose are powerful enough to kill a wolf. (Photograph © Bill Marchel)

Moose infested with winter ticks lose much of their hair by spring. The ticks can number 50,000 on a single moose and can thus weaken the animal by draining its blood. This problem is only one of many that can afflict moose and make them easier for wolves to kill. (Photograph © L. David Mech)

further study is needed in others. The above list points to the fact that it is through exploiting natural weaknesses in the deer population that wolves can find enough to eat. Thus, wolves spend much of their time seeking such situations, and chance plays a strong role in how often such situations exist.

A hard winter, then, is a bonanza for wolves, while a mild winter leaves them hungry. During an especially severe winter when deer are particularly vulnerable, wolves sometimes kill more than they can eat at the time, a phenomenon known as "surplus killing." During winter 1968–69 along the Canadian border lakes, I saw where wolves had killed several deer and eaten just a few bites out of their rumps. Surplus killing happens for only a few weeks every ten to twenty years.

Given that wolves must rely on the less-fit members of a deer herd—which are relatively rare—the ratio of deer to wolves must be high. If there were too few deer, there would be fewer less-fit individuals for wolves to find, and the wolves would die off. Thus, in most of the Minnesota wolf range, the ratio of wolves to deer is about one wolf for every 75 to 300 deer.

Competition for Human Hunters?

The high ratio of deer to wolves explains why wolves generally do not compete much with hunters for deer. Although wolves kill deer year-round and hunters only during a short season in fall, there are so many deer, and they are so productive, that the herd can support both wolves and hunters. While many hunters fail to believe this, I have had several tell me that they do not mind the wolves taking deer. "I get mine every year anyway," I have heard them explain.

However, it is also true that if hunters were allowed to take more deer through an increased limit, longer seasons, or more hunters, a point could be reached where wolves and hunters would compete more. In addition, where deer density is low because of poor habitat, severe winters, or both, competition between wolves and hunters is greatest.

An extreme example of what can happen due to changing circumstances was documented in the eastern part of the BWCAW, from about Snowbank Lake to Lake Saganaga, an area covering about 1,500 square miles (3,885 square km). This region of low fertility and the harshest winter weather in Minnesota supported a herd of deer year-round during the 1940s through the late 1960s. These deer were

For each wolf in Minnesota there are about 75 to 300 deer in the same area. Therefore, even with wolves killing deer year-round and human hunters taking deer for just a few days in fall, there is little competition between wolves and hunters. Only in the worst deer habitat in northeastern Minnesota is there evidence that, under present deer hunting regulation, wolves may compete with hunters. (Photograph © Bill Marchel)

favored by a period of mild winters as well as the young vegetation brought by logging and fires (see chapter 2). The state-sponsored wolf control, including bounties that didn't end until 1965, no doubt helped.

After logging was discontinued and when weather conditions reversed for several years beginning in 1968–69, the combination of the severe winters, the poor fertility and habitat of the area, and the recovered wolf population overwhelmed the deer herd. Year by year, as each hard winter hit, the wolves picked off the remaining deer. Now, more than twenty-five years later, there are still no wintering deer in this region, wolf density has also dropped, and the resident wolves feed mainly on moose and beavers.

Again, this was the worst case, and it happened in only a tiny fraction of Minnesota's wolf range. Elsewhere, in a fourteen-county area of the wolf's range, both hunter success and total harvest of deer increased even while the wolf population was expanding. Under the usual conditions and hunting regulations, then, wolves are rarely serious competitors with Minnesota deer hunters.

Wolf vs. Moose

Minnesota wolves that do not prey on deer rely on moose. Most everywhere moose live in Minnesota, so too do wolves. Thus, Minnesota wolves prey on moose to a greater or lesser extent depending on how many deer, beavers, and livestock also inhabit the specific area. In the eastern BWCAW, moose form the main prey of several packs, especially in winter when no deer live there. My colleague Mike Nelson has watched wolves actually jump on the back of a moose in a stream bed to attack it, one of the more bizarre methods of attack anyone has seen.

Although little direct study of wolf-moose interactions has been done in Minnesota, information

Above: To supplement their main diet of large hoofed animals, such as deer and moose, the wolf will eat almost any other kind of animal. Besides beavers, wolves will kill snowshoe hares, porcupines, squirrels, woodchucks, raccoons, skunks, and other smaller creatures, even mice. (Photograph © Michael H. Francis)

Right: When beavers come on to land to cut trees for food, they are especially vulnerable to wolves. The beaver's lifestyle of maintaining a stick and mud house surrounded by a moat helps protect them from wolves most of the time. However, when beavers build their dams to flood their ponds, they also risk being grabbed and eaten by a wolf. (Photograph © L. David Mech)

from nearby Isle Royale and other areas show what types of moose wolves tend to kill: calves, older moose, rutting bulls, malnourished individuals, and those debilitated by parasites, injuries, and other conditions. Despite predation by wolves and by bears (on newborn calves primarily), Minnesota still manages to hold a moose hunt at least every other year.

Wolf vs. Beaver

The third prey animal often taken by wolves is beaver. Beavers live throughout Minnesota wolf range, and at least from spring break-up until fall freeze-up, they supplement the wolf's diet. It is easy to see how the beaver's behavior of damming a stream to create a moat around its house is an adaptation for keeping safe from predators like wolves.

Still, beavers must venture onto land to cut trees for food, and wily wolves have learned to catch wary beavers some of these times. During spring in the BWCAW, I have often seen tracks in the snow where a beaver has emerged through a hole in the ice, waddled toward a tree to cut, and ended up as a nondescript patch of bloody snow after a wolf intercepted it. Again, certain more-vulnerable individuals, perhaps those taking unwarranted risks, are probably the types wolves most often catch.

Other beavers disperse from their natal ponds and sometimes must travel overland or in shallow streams or ditches to reach new waterways. Without plenty of deep water through which to escape, probably most of these beavers are doomed if wolves find them.

Other Potential Prey

The prey that gets wolves into the most trouble is domestic animals, primarily livestock, but also pet dogs. It is most distressing when people come home expecting their dog to greet them affectionately only to find it whimpering and limping from a severe gash or bite. Up to twenty-five dogs per year are reported killed by wolves in Minnesota, and the number is increasing as wolf ranges expand. Many dog kills are never reported because there is no compensation payment for pets, and the government cannot kill wolves

that preyed on dogs unless there are other dogs nearby that the wolves might also kill.

Wolves apparently regard hoofed livestock like any other prey—a ready source of food if they can overcome the livestock's strange habitat: fences and open pasture, accompanied by human sights, sounds, and smells. Although it may take up to a year for local wolves to learn how to deal with livestock's bizarre surroundings, too many do figure it out. "They have even learned to come right into the yard and kill calves next to the barn," one farmer told me.

Wolves also must contend with the defensive abilities of livestock, but as with other dangerous prey, they do so. For example, with cattle, wolves usually take calves. Sheep or turkeys, of course, are all vulnerable, so wolves often kill many at a time. (Fortunately not many sheep are raised in Minnesota's wolf range, and most turkeys are well fenced.) Every other type of livestock is also taken in Minnesota: horses, pigs, goats, chickens, and ducks.

There are probably few animals a wolf will not eat. Steve Fritts once saw tracks and fur remains where wolves had torn a skunk apart on a forest road. I have watched Minnesota wolves chase snowshoe hares, and in Alaska, some wolves live on salmon for certain periods. Porcupines are also prey for wolves. Any study that analyzes wolf scats turns up a wide variety of miscellaneous items.

Farley Mowat's 1963 work of fiction (and its 1983 movie adaptation) *Never Cry Wolf* had wolves subsisting exclusively on mice; although that was no more true than anything else in those presentations, wolves do eat mice, as well as squirrels, woodchucks, and various other vertebrates. About the only creature I have seen wolves pass up are shrews, which have obnoxious scent glands. (Wolves are intrigued by shrew scent, however. The most tracked-down area in the snow I have ever seen was in Fritts's study area where wolves had been trying to dig out of a deep snowy ditch a dead shrew in a beer bottle!)

Despite all the miscellaneous items that the wolf eats, these merely supplement the creature's main diet, which is almost always hoofed animals of some sort.

CHAPTER 8

Wolf Management in Minnesota
by Steven H. Fritts

Sharing our space with wildlife has its delights but also its challenges. Most everyone enjoys seeing deer, but when the whitetail has just nipped their prized tulips or leaped in front of their car, it becomes a problem. Similar examples could be given about bears, geese, squirrels, and other wildlife. The modern science of wildlife management assumes that it is usually in the best interest of both humans and wildlife to influence where animals live and how abundant they become.

The conflict with some animals, real or imagined, is greater than with others. The wolf has a great impact on the human psyche, as well as affecting people who rely on livestock for their livelihood. And because humans view the wolf with strong emotion, differences of opinion on whether and how wolves should be managed are inevitable.

Why Manage Wolves at All?
There are three possible reasons wolves need managing in Minnesota. First, wolves are perceived as a threat to people, especially children. Although the animals usually pose little danger to humans in Minnesota, a few incidents of wolves attacking children in Ontario and

Facing page: Wolves, like other wildlife, have their place in Minnesota, and Minnesotans are lucky to still have large expanses of wild land where such creatures can live. However, wolves sometimes cause conflict with humans by killing livestock and pets, frightening rural parents who are concerned about their young children, and causing some deer hunters to believe wolves are competing with them for deer. Thus, society has decided to manage wolf populations, although there remains much disagreement about precisely how. (Photograph © Michael H. Francis)
Inset: A wild gray wolf crosses the path of a wildlife surveillance camera set up on a Minnesota deer trail. Most wolf conflict with humans arises in semi-wild areas and agricultural regions. Here, usually at night or in early morning, wolves sometimes stalk cattle, sheep, turkeys, horses, and other livestock. Farmers cannot afford the time to wait up for wolves to appear and try to scare them away. Neither do fences or farm yards keep them out. (Photograph © Bill Marchel)

Figure 10

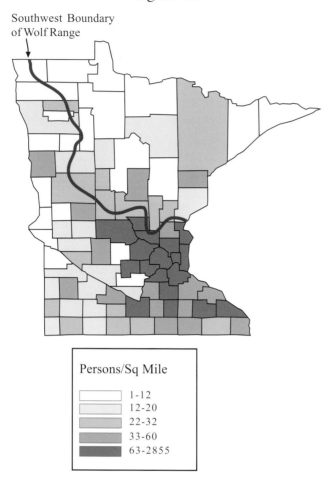

Southwest Boundary
of Wolf Range

Persons/Sq Mile

	1-12
	12-20
	22-32
	33-60
	63-2855

Figure 10: Human population distribution (as of 1990) and current Minnesota wolf range. (Wolf range data: Minnesota Department of Natural Resources. Population distribution data: U.S. Census Bureau, 1990 Decennial Census)

India lend some credence to people's fears. The increase in number and distribution of wolves in Minnesota during the past two decades has resulted in more wolves living near people than at any time in Minnesota's history (Figure 10). In addition, wolves may have less fear of humans than they did three decades ago when they were heavily persecuted. The potential for a wolf harming a human is therefore higher.

The most evident reason to manage wolves is their depredations on livestock and pets. Although such depredations affect a small percentage of farmers annually, some farmers can have serious losses. Failure to act against livestock-killing wolves would result in far higher losses in the future. People who lose pets, mainly dogs, to wolves are understandably irate, especially if the animal has been a longtime companion or is an expensive breed. Dealing with individual wolves that have killed livestock has been the predominant form of wolf management in Minnesota since the early 1970s.

A third possible reason for managing wolves would be to alleviate predation on Minnesota's deer herd. The issue of wolves killing deer has long been a hot topic in northern Minnesota and was used to justify the wolf bounty. Indeed, each wolf eats the equivalent of 15 to 20 adult-sized deer per year. Based on the Minnesota DNR's 1997–98 estimate of 2,450 wolves, that amounts to 36,000 to 50,000 deer per year. Yet that does not have to mean wolves compete with deer hunters, who harvest two to four times as many deer (see chapter 7). Habitat and weather have a far greater effect than predators on the state's deer numbers.

A History of the Wolf Management Debate
Management of wolves in Minnesota has ranged from attempting to eradicate them using every method available to giving them complete legal protection.

After the U.S. Secretary of the Interior classified the eastern timber wolf as "endangered" in 1967, Minnesota tried in vain to develop a state-wide wolf management plan for its wolves that would be acceptable to federal and state agencies and the public. The proposal suggested a harvest ceiling of 150 to 200 wolves per year with a five-and-a-half-month closed season. Even though the plan offered far more protection than the wolf had ever had, it was assailed by pro-wolf organizations for still allowing some killing of wolves. The Department of the Interior failed to endorse the plan, leaving the wolf without protection except in the Superior National Forest (see chapter 1).

In 1974, the gray wolf was listed as "endangered" throughout the lower forty-eight states under the federal Endangered Species Act of 1973 and given full protection. Killing a wolf was punishable by imprisonment for up to a year, a fine of up to $20,000, or both. Minnesota's Directed Predator Control Program (see chapter 1) was ended. Farmers or government agents could not even kill wolves to protect livestock. Farmers were not shy about voicing their unhappiness about their situation.

To people in northern Minnesota, it made no sense to declare the wolf endangered. In their neck of the woods there were "wolves aplenty." People outside northern Minnesota, especially from distant states that had long since lost their wolves, had a different view. Whether Minnesota's wolves were properly classified as "endangered" was a matter of human perspective.

Faced with its new responsibility, the U.S. Fish and Wildlife Service organized a small depredation-control program. In 1975, it began live-trapping wolves at or near farms where farmers complained of stock losses. The Brzoznowski farm near Orr was the site of much of this trapping. Because the wolves could not be killed, the Fish and Wildlife Service moved them to remote forested areas. Some wolves were caught before a depredation occurred and at distances up to five miles (8 km) from farms. In some instances, trapping continued for several weeks. Wolf advocates strongly criticized the program for its open-ended trapping. A number of the transplanted wolves returned to the Brzoznowski farm and resumed killing livestock.

On the advice of its recovery team, the Fish and Wildlife Service changed the Minnesota wolf's classification to "threatened" in 1978. This action allowed government personnel to euthanize wolves after they had committed "significant depredations on lawfully present domestic animals. . . ." A lawsuit and ruling by a federal judge gave additional guidance to the program. The judge restricted trapping to within a quarter mile of the farms where livestock had been killed or injured and forbade the killing of pups. In addition, the state legislature established a compensation program to pay farmers for livestock killed by wolves.

In 1979, the Fish and Wildlife Service transferred

One of the worst problems wolves can cause is attacks on pets, especially dogs. Wolves seem to be attracted to dogs, probably because they are so like wolves. It is even possible that wolves attack dogs just like they sometimes attack strange wolves in order to defend their territories. On the other hand, wolves often eat the pets they kill, which especially anguishes the pet owners. In Minnesota, about twenty-five dogs per year are reportedly killed by wolves. (Photograph © Layne Kennedy)

Viewpoints about wolves and wolf management in Minnesota and around the world differ between rural and urban residents, as this editorial cartoon demonstrates. As society becomes more urbanized, it grows more tolerant of wild creatures living in the countryside; however, rural residents who must contend directly with these creatures tend to be more wary of them. Resource managers must do their best to consider both types of attitudes. Minnesota is just beginning to go through the process of forging an ecologically and socially sound approach to wolf management now that its wolf population has recovered and will soon be removed from the federal Endangered Species List. (Cartoon © Kirk Anderson, St. Paul Pioneer Press)

the control program to its research division under L. David Mech. At this time I was finishing a Ph.D. program at the University of Minnesota that involved studying wolves recolonizing northwestern Minnesota. I was hired to operate the program at the field level, and Bill Paul (already with the program) became my assistant.

Headquartered in Grand Rapids, Paul, our seasonal biologists, and I trapped depredating wolves under the guidelines imposed by court decisions and several conditions Mech instituted. Wolves could only be trapped if there were wounded livestock or carcass remains and evidence that wolves caused the damage. Also we could trap for only short periods. These rules were to ensure that wolves were captured only in response to livestock or pets actually being attacked and to maximize chances that any wolves caught were

the guilty ones.

Early in the program, we supplemented trapping with various non-lethal methods. We hung surveyors' flagging on fences and trees in an attempt to mimic Europeans' use of similar "fladre" to funnel wolves while hunting them. Farmers laughed and cows ate the flagging. We also placed flashing lights and strobe light-sirens in and along perimeters of pastures, tried taste aversion conditioning via lithium-chloride-laced baits, and encouraged farmers to use guard dogs. All but taste aversion seemed to have some effect in some circumstances, but none worked as well as or as consistently as trapping and euthanizing problem wolves.

We also discouraged farmers from leaving dead livestock in fields, pasturing livestock in densely wooded or brushy areas, and allowing calving and

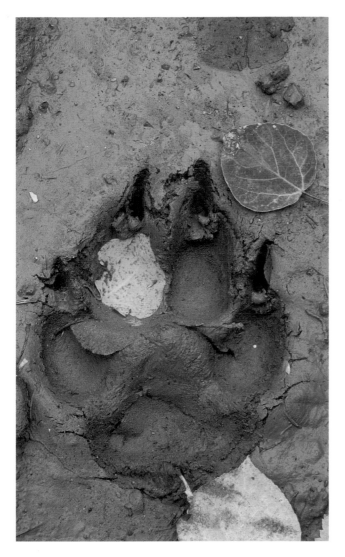

Ever since the wolf in Minnesota was downlisted from endangered to threatened in 1978, the federal government has conducted a wolf-control program. When evidence of wolves killing livestock has been found, such as wolf tracks around eaten cow remains, federal government agents try to catch and kill the wolves that did the damage. (Photograph © Lynn & Donna Rogers)

When a Minnesota farmer finds a domestic animal that has apparently been killed or injured by wolves, he notifies the U.S. Department of Agriculture (USDA) Wildlife Services program. If an investigating biologist finds evidence that wolves were involved, the biologist sets traps to catch the offending wolf or wolves. Any wolves caught there are then euthanized. The program is designed to minimize the number of wolves taken and yet reduce chances for additional depredations. (Photograph © Layne Kennedy)

Wildlife Services' biologists have tried many non-lethal techniques to minimize livestock depredations, but none have worked well or consistently. Techniques included guard dogs, blinking highway flashers, strobe lights, fence flagging, and chemical-aversive conditioning. The federal government has spent millions of dollars during the past thirty years similarly trying to find non-lethal techniques to prevent coyote depredations on livestock, also to little avail. (Photograph © Steven H. Fritts)

lambing in remote pastures, thinking these practices might predispose livestock to wolf depredations. (A study done since then questions whether any of these practices has much effect, however.) In addition, we radio-collared wolves around farming communities to learn how much time they spent near livestock.

Farmers were not exactly jovial when they called to report livestock killed. One morning I arrived at our Grand Rapids office a few minutes late and noticed a green phone slip taped to my door. Those slips almost always meant trouble. This one read, "Call from Emil _____! Calf killed this morning! Call or get out there quick! He's going to shoot at everything that moves!"

Nor were farmers in the best mood when one of us showed up. I usually sent Paul or one of the trappers out to investigate. As representatives of the federal government, they were often the object of the farmers' frustrations about everything from the Endangered Species Act to high taxes and big govern-ment. But we tried to be understanding since the farmers had just suffered a financial loss, and federal law kept them from taking action against the animal responsible.

At that time (mid-1970s) no one knew how many livestock wolves actually killed. People who disliked wolves generally thought the number was high; people who liked wolves thought the opposite. No one had kept records until our program began or even examined alleged depredations with a critical eye. During the first two years of our program, 1979 and 1980, verified losses averaged 17 cattle, 28 sheep, 28 turkeys, and 1 dog at just fifteen farms. The state paid farmers an annual average of $20,616 total for those losses.

In the years to follow, wolves settled in new areas and their populations increased. Their adaptability amazed us. They were willing to live in more open areas and closer to higher densities of people and roads than we had imagined. They also killed more

Above: Once government agents set traps around farms where wolf depredations have been confirmed, they place signs to warn against letting pets run freely in the area. Usually traps are left out until wolves are caught or for seven to ten days if they are not caught. The assumption is made that usually if wolves are not caught during this time, they probably are not a further threat to livestock in that area. (Photograph © Layne Kennedy)

Left: Wolves trapped by federal trappers around farms where they have killed domestic animals are euthanized. In recent years, as the Minnesota wolf population has increased and expanded its range into agricultural areas, some 150 to 200 wolves per year have had to be killed. (Photograph © Steven H. Fritts)

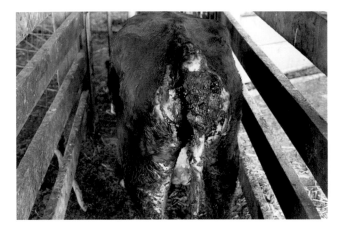

When wolves attack cattle, the carnivores tend to bite them from behind. If an attacked cow is not killed, the wounds must be treated. The Minnesota Department of Agriculture compensates livestock owners for livestock killed or wounded by wolves. Compensation payments have increased from $21,000 in 1980 to $65,000 in 1999. (Photograph © Steven H. Fritts)

Figure 11

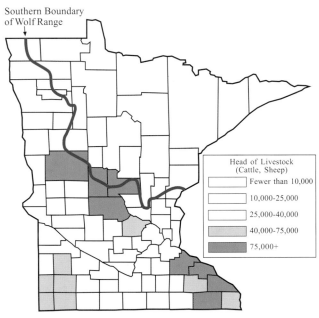

Figure 11: Minnesota wolf range and livestock distribution. (Wolf range data: Minnesota Department of Natural Resources. Livestock distribution data: Minnesota Agriculture Statistics Service)

livestock. For the five-year period of 1993 to 1997, wolves killed an average of 75 cattle, 22 sheep, 728 turkeys, and 9 dogs per year. The livestock losses occurred at seventy-one farms and resulted in compensation payments of $37,300 per year total.

Verified losses were still below 1 percent of the livestock in wolf range, although actual losses likely were higher than we verified. Farmers were not always able to produce the kind of evidence we required. The control program, which Congress moved to the U.S. Department of Agriculture in 1986 and is now ably directed by Bill Paul, killed an average of 152 wolves per year during that five-year period, at a cost of about $1,225 per wolf.

In 1983, the Fish and Wildlife Service and its wolf recovery team recommended that trappers be allowed to kill up to fifty wolves on a preventive basis in areas of chronic depredations and that the control program be turned over to the state. Wolf protection groups sued the government, and a court order forbade the change.

Successful Recovery Sparks New Issues

The goal of the Endangered Species Act of 1973 is to protect populations of endangered species until they recover to the point of no longer being threatened or endangered, then remove them from the endangered species list and allow states to manage them. The wolf recovery team of the U.S. Fish and Wildlife Service set a population goal of 1,250 to 1,400 wolves for Minnesota. The Minnesota Department of Natural Resources (DNR) has shown that the population now exceeds the recovery plan's goal by a thousand or more wolves, and most population expansion in the past decade has been in areas with more people and more farms (Figure 11). Therefore, the increase in wolf problems should not be surprising.

There is every reason to believe that numbers of livestock killed will continue to rise as long as the wolf population does (Figure 12). So will compensation payments (which totaled $730,000 through 1999). And so will the calls from worried moms whose children wait for the school bus near where wolves live. Decisions will have to be made about how to deal with these problems as management authority returns to the Minnesota DNR.

Much has changed over the years that will affect the future management of wolves. The wolf's public approval rating has soared, even to the point of the creature becoming a symbol of the natural world. Many organizations promote the wolf and try to

Hunting wolves is very difficult because they are rarely seen. That is why wolf control is most often done by trapping or snaring. Even these methods are very time consuming, and wolf fur is currently not very valuable. Thus, most hunters and trappers would only seek wolves if fur prices increased considerably, or if they were paid incentives for their efforts. (Photograph © Michael H. Francis)

Figure 12

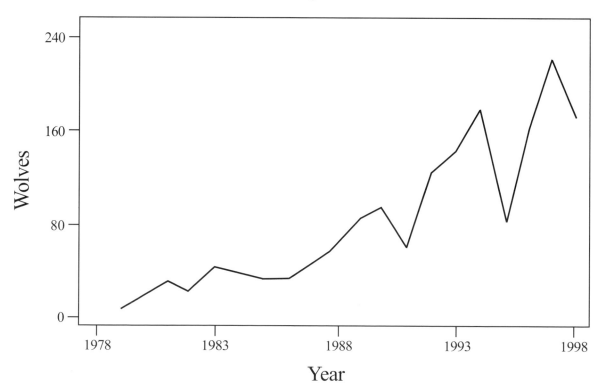

Figure 12: Trend in number of Minnesota wolves killed by the U.S. Department of Agriculture for livestock-depredation control. (Data: U.S. Department of Agriculture)

assure that it remains protected. Some have long used the plight of the wolf in their fund-raising campaigns. The media likes to hype the controversy that surrounds the wolf.

In addition, human populations have become more urbanized, and urban and rural folks are not always sympathetic to each other's concerns. The animal rights movement is strengthening; the popularity of traditional outdoor activities, such as hunting and trapping, is declining. Proven methods of wolf control (traps, snares, hunting, poison) are now less acceptable. Some people believe it is morally wrong to kill wolves. Thus, while wolf-human conflicts are on the rise in Minnesota, there seems to be little public agreement on how to deal with them.

Of the reasons to manage Minnesota's wolves, depredation on livestock is the most compelling. No solution to this problem is in sight that does not include the killing of problem wolves. Millions of dollars have been spent trying to solve a very similar problem—coyote depredations—without a suitable non-lethal solution.

Some people wonder why farmers make such a fuss about wolves since the farmers get paid for their losses. The reason is that not all livestock killed can be found, and farmers do not always receive full value. They must fill out forms and deal with the government; lost time and aggravation are not compensated. The check can take months to arrive. Compensation offers no permanent fix for the depredation problem. Having to increase payouts that result from more wolves could ultimately result in political opposition to the state's compensation program.

Current Wolf Management Options

What options are available for managing Minnesota's wolves after the wolf is "delisted" and the state DNR regains management authority? One option is for the federal government to continue to control wolves as before. A variation would be for controllers to do preventive control by capturing wolves over winter or in spring in areas of chronic depredations before losses occur. Or the Minnesota DNR could capture and kill wolves in areas of chronic losses and perhaps in broad areas of the state where wolves are most likely to cause problems. This option is expensive and time consuming, but it would reduce livestock losses and conflict.

The other major option is to involve the public,

which could happen through allowing the legal shooting of wolves by licensed sportspersons in specified areas at certain times of the year. Hunting could be permitted only near areas with chronic depredation problems, in places where other kinds of wolf-human conflicts are occurring, or in the more southerly and westerly counties where wolf presence would cause the most problems. However, deliberate hunting of wolves is difficult; most would probably be shot by deer hunters who just happen to see a wolf.

Trapping of wolves for their fur like Canada and Alaska allow could also be tried, but interest in trapping depends on the price of fur, which fluctuates greatly. In addition, most expertise in trapping wolves was lost during the long period of federal protection. Trapping by the public has not been very effective in controlling wolf populations in Canada in recent years because the number of trappers with the necessary skill has been too low.

Some wolf advocates strongly oppose public hunting and trapping wolves, preferring that all killing be done by government agents. Other people respond with "A dead wolf is a dead wolf; why does it matter who kills it?" The 1999 Kellert survey found that more than two-thirds of the Minnesota public preferred to have hunters and trappers take wolves rather than government controllers.

Another change would be to allow livestock owners to shoot or trap wolves on their property, either with some restrictions or without. In reality, the chance of a farmer seeing a wolf is low, and few have the time and skill to trap them. Farmers would kill very few wolves, but any they did kill on their property would likely be potential transgressors. Having the freedom to protect their property would mean a great deal to farmers' peace of mind and feelings of self-determination. It might also relieve some of the anti-wolf and anti-government feelings among farmers. Wolf protectionists believe, however, that allowing landowners to kill depredating wolves would result in innocent wolves being killed.

Any of the above scenarios involve different rules in different places. This raises the concept of zoning. Hypothetically, wolves could be allowed to live in some zones (e.g., the wilderness) with no control by people. They could be actively prevented from occupying other zones (e.g., counties with intensive livestock production). And they could be subject to closely regulated hunting and trapping in others (e.g.,

WOLF MANAGEMENT QUIZ: CAN YOU FIND THE MIDDLE GROUND BETWEEN WHAT THE TWO SIDES WANT?

kanderson@pioneerpress.com KIRK

a.) LIVING

b.) DEAD

Proposals for managing wolves in recent years have been contentious because people who feel strongly about wolves have gained the most attention. Extreme viewpoints have ranged from those considering the life of each wolf sacred to those proposing to eliminate all wolves. The views of most Minnesotans, however, are far more middle-of-the-road. (Cartoon © Kirk Anderson, St. Paul Pioneer Press)

areas bordering livestock production).

This zoning approach could hold promise for preserving unmolested populations in parts of Minnesota where wolves are less likely to get into trouble while reducing their numbers in places with lots of livestock and people. Obviously, the larger the zones, the easier it would be for the DNR to enforce its regulations. Actually, a simple zoning system was recommended by the U.S. Fish and Wildlife Service's wolf recovery team and has been in partial effect for several years. For example, wolves in extreme northeastern Minnesota are not killed when they attack livestock and pets. Wolf protection groups reject zoning because it would give less protection to wolves in some zones.

Public Input is Critical

Those of us who have worked to make sure the wolf survives in Minnesota have long been called unprint-

able names by anti-wolf people. Now we are also criticized by those who object to any form of wolf control. (Thus, the thick skins we joke about wearing must do double duty.) Nevertheless, some degree of management of Minnesota's thriving wolf population is absolutely essential, or the public will take matters into its own hands. The public's desires will ultimately determine how that is done. More public education about wolves would be helpful because better understanding of wolves tends to reduce extreme points of view.

Hopefully, the citizens of Minnesota will be able to reach a compromise ensuring that this marvelous animal will always be a part of the Minnesota north woods while being respectful of and responsive to the needs of folks who are negatively affected by wolves. Reasonable people should be able to work out such a compromise.

Attitudes of Minnesotans about Wolves

How do Minnesota citizens feel about the wolf, and how do they want to manage this controversial creature? The answers to these questions are as complex as the animal they address. A 1999 survey by Stephen R. Kellert of Yale University, sponsored by the International Wolf Center, adds a great deal of information about the attitudes of Minnesotans about wolves.

Minnesota citizens are in strong agreement that they care about their wolves: 80 percent of Minnesotans show a positive attitude, including 60 percent of livestock raisers. Furthermore, 70 percent of farmers and 80 percent of Minnesotans in general believe that wolves add a great deal to the wilderness experience.

However, on one of the most important management issues—whether wolves should be allowed to inhabit all of Minnesota or just their current range—Minnesotans are about evenly split. This split is also reflected in the attitudes of the public about hunting and trapping wolves.

Probably some of the reluctance of people who disapprove of wolf hunting or trapping results from the fact that more than half of Minnesotans believe that such taking might endanger the wolf again. However, as indicated in chapters 1 and 8, it was not regulated harvesting of wolves that endangered them. Rather, it was wholesale persecution, especially poisoning, den digging, aerial hunting, and a year-around open season; regulated hunting and trapping just takes the surplus wolves each year.

Additional evidence of misunderstanding the wolf situation in Minnesota comes from responses to a question about how many wolves the state should have. Pluralities of farmers and general Minnesota citizens thought that the minimum number of wolves that the federal wolf recovery team prescribed for the state—1,250—was about right or too many. Because the state already harbors far more wolves than that—2,450 in winter 1997–98—this implies that most citizens should not favor expansion of the wolf population and probably should favor reducing wolf numbers.

Interestingly, farmers understand all this much better than non-farmers. In fact, livestock producers were significantly more knowledgeable about wolves than were non-farmers, according to Kellert's survey. For example, 72 percent of farmers correctly answered a question about how wolves kill prey, whereas only 51 percent of non-northern Minnesotans answered correctly. This was typical of the difference in replies to Kellert's questions regarding citizens' knowledge about wolves.

One of the biggest differences in attitudes between southern Minnesota residents and farmers involved questions about whether wolves that prey on livestock should be killed. Only 38 percent of downstaters agreed with the proposal while 83 percent of farmers agreed.

Despite this difference over hunting and trapping wolves, there was wide agreement that if wolves needed to be destroyed, it was better for sport hunters and fur trappers to kill them than the government.

Given all these attitudinal cross-currents, it will be a special challenge for the Minnesota legislature and the DNR to finally forge a wolf management plan that will best meet society's needs and will minimize public discord.

Kellert Survey (1999), Selected Results

1. Question: Overall, how much do you care about wolves?

	Non-north	North	Farmers
Care	79%	78%	79%
Do not	21%	22%	21%

2. Question: Does the presence of wolves add a great deal to a wilderness experience in Minnesota?

	Yes		No	
	1985*	1999	1985*	1999
Non-north	63	91	16	6
North	54	81	27	12
Farmers	42	71	35	25
Hunters	50	83	31	14
Trappers	60	78	28	18

*Based on a similar survey by Kellert in 1985.

3. Question: Should wolves be allowed to spread throughout Minnesota?

	Non-north	North	Farmers
Yes	44%	46%	17%
No	45%	49%	70%

4. Question: What do you think about the federal Wolf Recovery Team's conclusion that Minnesota should have a minimum of 1,250 wolves for five years after delisting?

	Non-north	North	Farmers
About right or too many	40%	49%	53%
Too few	20%	19%	9%
No opinion	40%	32%	38%

5. Question: Do you believe hunting or trapping wolves will make them rare?

	Non-north	North	Farmers
Yes	56%	55%	23%
No	38%	43%	71%

6. Question: If Minnesota wolves are abundant and well managed, should people be allowed to hunt or trap them?

	Non-north	North	Farmers
Yes	46%	56%	78%
No	46%	40%	18%

7. Question: Should wolves that kill livestock be eliminated?

	Non-north	North	Farmers
Yes	38%	71%	83%
No	47%	23%	11%

8. Question: For wolf control, would you prefer sport hunting or fur trapping rather than government taking?

	Non-north	North	Farmers
Yes	66%	70%	76%
No	20%	21%	9%

9. Question: Are you afraid of wolves?

	Yes	No
Non-north	42%	53%
North	36%	60%
Farmers	30%	65%
Hunters	27%	69%
Trappers	27%	73%

CHAPTER 9

The International Wolf Center
by L. David Mech

*"The International Wolf Center supports the survival of the wolf
around the world by teaching about its life, its association
with other species and its dynamic relationships to humans."*
—Mission statement of the International Wolf Center

The International Wolf Center differs from all the many other wolf-oriented organizations by advocating for the wolf only through public education—no picketing, no lawsuits, no letter-writing campaigns, as helpful as they can sometimes be. Its philosophy is that by disseminating accurate, objective information about the wolf, it will best foster ecologically and socially sound wolf recovery and management in the long term.

However, the establishment of the International Wolf Center was almost as embattled and controversial as the wolf itself.

Public Interest Inspires Exhibits

As I studied wolves in northeastern Minnesota over the years, I received frequent calls from members of the public. They wanted information, wished to go into the field with us, or hoped to see kill remains, dens, or wolves from the air. It was, of course, impossible to accommodate all these requests, but I did understand and appreciate the public's interest. Often when a teacher or professor would call, or a museum group, zoological society, or similar organization, I would try to cooperate.

Facing page: The International Wolf Center (IWC) is a Minnesota non-profit organization dedicated to disseminating objective information about the wolf. The International Wolf Center's 10,000 members from around the world, its staff of twenty, and its annual operating budget of over $1 million, is testimony to the public's interest in the wolf. The IWC operates a visitors' center in Ely, Minnesota. (Photograph © Deborah Sussex)
Inset: The International Wolf Center's logo is adopted from a famous Jacques' painting of wolves running on a lake in front of a cedar swamp.

Above: The International Wolf Center's "Wolves and Humans" exhibit examines many aspects of human interest in the wolf, including wolf myths, legends, and fairy tales, as well as the wolf in early and recent literature, art, and music. (Photograph © the International Wolf Center)

Right: Much of the IWC's "Wolves and Humans" exhibit deals with facts about basic wolf biology. Thus, displays include replications of remains of actual wolf-killed prey, including livestock. Physical problems that make prey vulnerable to wolves are illustrated with the actual bones showing various types of disabilities. (Photograph © Dan Grandmaison)

IWC board member Nancy Gibson (left) and educator Amy Kay Kerber use live "ambassador" wolves at special International Wolf Center presentations to give the audience a look at an animal that few people ever see in the wild. There are few better ways of stimulating the public's interest in learning more about wolves than actually seeing such an animal. (Photograph © O. J. Volkman)

Clearly there was strong demand and interest for wolf information and for interacting in the field with wolves. Furthermore, the wolf has always been a misunderstood and controversial animal, so there has forever been a strong need for the dissemination of accurate information about the creature. All of the federal government's wolf recovery plans emphasized the need for objective public information about wolves.

Thus, I had long had an idea that some sort of private organization could thrive in our area by meeting such needs and interests. An occasion to promote this idea arose in 1972 when the Superior National Forest, a local division of the U.S. Forest Service, commissioned me to prepare a wolf-management plan. In the section on information and education needs, I elaborated upon this idea. I recommended that the displays in the National Forest Service's Voyageur's Visitor Center in Ely be devoted to various wolf themes, and I listed several display possibilities: maps, charts, photos, mounted wolves, and hardware associated with wolf biology and research. The idea was not only to provide information to the public but also to promote the presence of the wolf in the area. The report, however, sat on the shelf unheeded.

About ten years later, the Science Museum of Minnesota sought my opinion about creating a temporary wolf exhibit for its museum in St. Paul. Of course, I endorsed the idea. When the museum folks also asked what to include in the exhibit, I merely pulled out my report, photocopied the information and education section, and sent it to them. Follow-up discussions led me to become their chief consultant for the exhibit. To broaden the scope of the project and gather additional ideas, I suggested various colleagues to be included on the committee for the exhibit. We held several brainstorming sessions, and certain members agreed to develop ideas within their own specialty. For example, my former student Fred

A new wolf-viewing auditorium was added to the 17,000-square-foot (1,530-square-m) International Wolf Center in 1998. This auditorium allows visitors to sit and observe a pack of three live wolves as they interact with each other, feed on deer carcasses, and demonstrate various other kinds of wolf behavior. The addition of two white Arctic wolves is planned for summer 2000. (Photograph © the International Wolf Center)

Harrington, who had done his Ph.D. study on wolf howling in the Ely area, helped develop a special howling booth as well as an audio tape on wolf howling.

The Science Museum had obtained a large grant from the National Endowment for the Humanities to build the exhibit and to send it to six other museums after its display ended in St. Paul. The museum did an excellent job creating a 7,000-square-foot (630-square-m) exhibit called "Wolves and Humans." It was an instant success, and after its six-month stint in St. Paul, the exhibit was sent to Yellowstone National Park. There it helped pave the way for the reintroduction of wolves into the Park. Several more venues for the exhibit followed, including Boise, Idaho; New York City; Washington, D.C.; Dallas–Fort Worth, Texas; Montreal, Quebec; Green Bay, Wisconsin; Davis, California; Vancouver, British Columbia; Anchorage, Alaska; and even Honolulu,

Hawaii, which never even had any wolves. Altogether the exhibit was seen by two-and-one-half-million people.

Exhibit's Success Fosters Idea for Center

When the Science Museum informed me that, unless some special use could be found for the exhibit after its last venue, they would dismantle it, I immediately recognized the opportunity to use the exhibit as a lever to develop a wolf center.

I explained my idea to the various wolf advocates, and several agreed to help me. Our group organized and incorporated in 1985, added a variety of new members, and became the Committee for an International Wolf Center.

Our plan was to use the gift of the exhibit, valued at about $500,000 at the time, to leverage funds from various granting agencies, governmental bodies, and private benefactors who might be interested.

Visitors to the International Wolf Center can watch a captive wolf pack and listen to its piped-in howls. The wolves were born in 1993, so are excellent examples of mature wolves. The IWC's captive wolves have enough room to break into a full run and chase each other around their pen without feeling hemmed in. A $55,000 set of improvements currently underway will include a pond and a small stream where the wolves can cool off in the summer. (Photograph © Lynn & Donna Rogers)

In addition, we thought we could obtain incentives from different towns that might compete for the wolf center.

Selecting a Site

From the start we wanted the center somewhere in Minnesota wolf range. This was to demonstrate that the wolf had a positive, nonconsumptive economic value in addition to the value of its pelt and in contrast to the negative impact of its depredation on livestock.

We notified the northern Minnesota communities in wolf range that they could compete to become the home of the International Wolf Center. The name "International" was added to the Wolf Center concept because of my chairmanship of the World Conservation Union's (IUCN) Wolf Specialist Group, an organization of wolf authorities from around the world. My long association with the wolf group would ensure that I could call upon specialists from abroad to advise on the project, to visit the center, and tell audiences about the wolf in their own countries to help broaden the appeal of the center.

Four Minnesota communities submitted strong proposals for the center. The committee spent three days traveling to each of the cities, meeting with local officials, viewing potential center sites, and examining statistics on visitation rates, tourism facilities, and several other factors.

The Committee for an International Wolf Center did an elaborate analysis of the advantages that each of the four main contending cities had to offer. After much discussion, the committee chose Ely. Not only was Ely right in the heart of wolf range, but also it was where most of the state's wolf research had been conducted both historically and currently. Both elements would serve the center well in its planned programs and field trips.

Top, left: At 101 pounds (46 kg), Lakota is the largest of the IWC's resident wolves. (Photograph © Lynn & Donna Rogers)

Top, right: MacKenzie, the IWC pack's alpha female, is its only black wolf, adding an element of variety to the pack. Some wild packs also contain both gray wolves and black wolves. (Photograph © Lynn & Donna Rogers)

Bottom, right: Lucas is the only male member of the IWC's resident pack. Both he and Lakota, one of the pack's two females, have black, brown, and cream colors in their coats. (Photograph © Lynn & Donna Rogers)

Once Ely was chosen, Governor Rudy Perpich, who was much in favor of the center, flew to Ely on the following Saturday night and offered state help to build "the best wolf center" we could. Seed funding for the project came quickly from the Iron Range Resources Rehabilitation Board. Those funds allowed the committee to continue its planning, including architectural work.

However, progress in the state legislature went more slowly. In 1986, the House of Representatives granted some $3.8 million for the center, but because there was no companion bill in the Senate, the House bill died in conference committee.

Almost coincident with the legislative setback came a feasibility study report that said Ely may not have a high enough visitation rate to support the wolf center and recommended that the Committee for an International Wolf Center reopen its site-selection process. It did so, but after committee members visited sites and heard presentations by local proponents, they voted again to choose Ely for the site.

Because in 1987 the legislature was not considering the type of bonding bill that could have included the wolf center during that session, the committee was seeking an appropriation to help it continue planning and operating. It was granted $150,000 with the proviso that a legislative committee be allowed to review its site-selection process.

When the special legislative site-selection committee heard testimony from the wolf center committee as well as from its detractors, it decided unanimously that the wolf center committee had followed the proper process. The wolf center committee was free to continue garnering support for the center in Ely.

The Battle for Funds

In 1988, the wolf center committee opened an interim wolf center in the U.S. Forest Service's Voyageur Visitor's Center just east of Ely. It housed a few displays, dispensed literature, and featured captive wolves—just a slight teaser of things to come.

During the legislative session in 1990, the Committee for an International Wolf Center held an international wolf symposium in St. Paul. It was attended by about 300 people, including wolf authorities from around the globe. The Minnesota state legislature invited the international wolf specialists to a session, where all joined in an international wolf howl.

A few days later, the committee's request for $1.8 million reached the House-Senate Conference Com-

The International Wolf Center's captive wolves are so comfortable in their quarters that they come right up to the viewing windows, allowing visitors to see them up close and snap their pictures. Seeing the wolves safely yet close-up through the windows, children of all ages thrill to their first view of a real live wolf. The wolves seem to love it too. (Photograph © Lynn & Donna Rogers)

International Wolf Center staff members discuss the live wolves with rapt audiences. The attention that the wolves foster allows lecturers to present a wide variety of information. Questions abound, and the staff tries to answer them all or to suggest reliable sources where answers can be found. (Photograph © Dan Grandmaison)

mittee. Intensive, overnight lobbying by wolf center board member Nancy Gibson and pro-bono lobbyist Ellen Sampson succeeded in obtaining an appropriation of $1.2 million—a bittersweet victory. After having scaled back the project from a $3.8-million building to a $1.8-million building, it was disconcerting to have the legislature further scale back the funding from $1.8 to $1.2 million.

The wolf center committee felt that $1.8 million was the minimal requirement for the center. I will never forget a phone call I received from Nancy Gibson.

"What should I do?" she asked. "They only want to give us $1 million."

Instantly I replied, "Nancy, never turn down a million dollars."

As it was, Gibson was eventually able to persuade the conference committee to add another $200,000 to the appropriation. This addition was critical because the wolf center committee would have to raise the extra money from the private sector, and the addition of $200,000 made the task much more possible.

The wolf center board immediately set out to raise the additional money. A major contribution from local philantropist and environmentalist Wallace Dayton greatly assisted the fund-raising effort. Several years later, the Minnesota legislature would grant another $750,000 to complete a second phase of the building, including a 120-seat auditorium from which to view a captive wolf pack.

In addition, a life-size bronze sculpture of five running wolves, valued at $75,000, was donated for the wolf center grounds by wolf patron Valerie Gates of Denver, Colorado.

As the financial resources were secured, the committee had to face the additional complication of how to gain the proper legal status for the land where the wolf center would be built. As part of Ely's bid for the center, the U.S. Forest Service had offered to the committee the Voyageur's Visitors Center and surrounding land on which to build the center. However, when the time came, the committee discovered there was no legal way that could be done. Thus, the committee had to raise more funds, buy land elsewhere, and trade that land to the Forest Service for the Forest Service land it needed. Then, since state money would be used to build the center, the land

had to be donated to the state, specifically to the Minnesota Department of Natural Resources.

Meanwhile, a new governor had been elected, and he decided to freeze the bonding money the previous legislature had approved, including that for building the wolf center. After considerable lobbying by Nancy Gibson, however, Governor Arne Carlson released the wolf center's money.

Architectural plans soon gave way to construction of a 17,000-square-foot (1,530-square-m) building that incorporated the U.S. Forest Service's Voyageur's Visitor Center on a hill just east of Ely. It seemed fitting that the year before, a wolf pack had killed a deer in the field in front of the visitor's center, and that during groundbreaking, wolf howling was heard in reply to the joyous howls of wolf center enthusiasts. (No one ever knew that those replies came from my research project volunteers hidden back in the woods.)

The Wolf Center Opens Its Doors

The International Wolf Center opened the doors of its new building in June 1993, and like the "Wolves and Humans" exhibit, it too was an immediate success. Executive Director Walter Medwid took over in September 1993, and he and a staff of about twenty have very ably operated the center ever since. Between visitation and membership fees and retail sales and donations, the center has been able to make its operating budget of over $1 million each year. This in turn has allowed the center to carry on its mission in many different ways.

Each year some 40,000 to 50,000 people visit the International Wolf Center and view the "Wolves and Humans" exhibit and a captive wolf pack. Many also attend various field trips, including special excursions to howl to wild wolves. More than 9,000 members receive *International Wolf*, an authoritative, thirty-two-page quarterly magazine, and in 1998, the center's website (www.wolf.org) had 320,000 visits.

Not only does the International Wolf Center fulfill its intended role of being the world's foremost provider of objective information about wolves, but it also demonstrates the value of wolves to the public.

It also enhances the local economy; a University of Minnesota study showed that each year the International Wolf Center adds an estimated $3 million and sixty-five full-time jobs to the Ely area economy. No wonder. The International Wolf Center has hosted delegations from Denmark, England, France, Germany, Israel, Japan, Romania, and Sweden all wanting to start a similar institution in their countries.

The Future of Minnesota's Wolves

As the myriad of visitors to the International Wolf Center demonstrate, wolves are popular and valuable to many people around the world. In Minnesota, that popularity has succeeded in quadrupling wolf range and numbers in less than thirty years. The popularity has also masked the wolf's downside and imposed a burden on many inhabitants of wolf range.

Can Minnesotans, soon to be charged with responsibility for intelligently and rationally managing wolves, succeed in striking a compromise that is not only ecologically sound but socially sound as well?

The magnificent animal that is the wolf deserves no less.

Facing page, top: The International Wolf Center held its grand opening in June 1993—a welcome culmination of eight years of hard work by a volunteer board of directors. Biologists, naturalists, educators, explorers, business people, architects, and other board members all pitched in to help raise funds for the center. Some 40,000 to 50,000 people pass through the center each year. (Photograph © the International Wolf Center)

Facing page, bottom: Some of the International Wolf Center's most popular programs are its field trips. Visitors can sign up for field trips to examine wolf kill remains, tracks, and scats; to howl to wild wolves; and even to try to see wild wolves from an aircraft. Here biologist Mike Nelson guides such a trip. (Photograph © the International Wolf Center)

APPENDIX

Minnesota's Deer and Moose

Figure 13

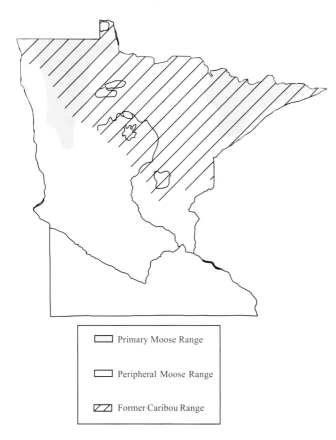

Primary Moose Range

Peripheral Moose Range

Former Caribou Range

Figure 13: Present range of moose and former range of caribou in Minnesota. (Data from the Minnesota Department of Natural Resources and Todd K. Fuller, 1986.)

The biology of the deer and moose that Minnesota wolves eat is as important to an understanding of the wolf as basic wolf biology itself. The lives of the wolf, deer, and moose are so intertwined that features of each are readily explained by their interactions with the others. This appendix, describing the lives of deer and moose, helps provide insight into those interactions.

Natural History of Deer in Minnesota
by Glenn D. DelGiudice

Minnesota's white-tailed deer currently are more abundant than ever, living throughout the state. However, over the years, their numbers and distribution have undergone dramatic changes. In 1909, Seton's map of the late prehistoric/early historic distribution of white-tailed deer across North America showed Minnesota at the northern limit of their range.

Before European settlement (1860), deer were most common in the hardwood forests of central and southeastern Minnesota, and rare in the conifer forests of the northeast.

During the late 1800s and early 1900s, logging, fire, and agriculture increasingly altered or cleared much of these old forests and stimulated young growth. This improved the area as deer habitat. By 1920, deer had become common in the forest zone, expanding their range as far as Canada.

Since the 1950s, forest deer populations have fluctuated with variations in winter severity, habitat, hunting, and wolf predation. In 1971, the Minnesota Department of Natural Resources set local population goals, and annual harvests were managed on a local level. From 1976 to 1995, Minnesota's forest deer populations increased steadily.

During the historically severe winter of 1995–96, as I studied deer in north-central Minnesota, we observed relatively high losses of deer in the state's northern forests, and low reproductive success the following spring. The record mild winter of 1997–

98 and relatively high reproductive success during 1998, greatly helped recovery of the northern deer herd. The deer population in Minnesota's wolf range in 1999 was estimated at 482,000.

Size, Weight, and Growth

As with all species, genetics largely dictates the wide variation in size of deer. But from fetal development to full-grown adult, size and weight are also strongly influenced by the pronounced seasonality of food abundance, availability, and quality. Newborn fawns weigh four to thirteen pounds (2 to 6 kg), with females attaining maximum weight in four years and males in five to six years.

The probability of fawn mortality increases with birth weights near the low end of this range. With most of a doe's pregnancy coinciding with winter, severe weather and poor nutrition can impose great challenge to her and to the development and survivability of her young. Following the severe winter of 1996–97, fellow researchers and I located newborn fawns that ranged from underdeveloped, stillborn twins weighing five and a half pounds (2 kg) each to live individuals weighing seven to thirteen pounds (3 to 6 kg).

Body length of adult does typically ranges from 61 to 84 inches (155 to 213 cm), and weight, 88 to 297 pounds (40 to 135 kg), although does weighing more than 160 pounds (73 kg) are considered large. Adult bucks are only slightly taller than does, with a shoulder height of about 36 inches (91 cm) and a belly height above ground of 20 inches (51 cm). Exceptionally large males weigh up to 385 pounds (175 kg).

Reproduction

With white-tailed deer, only males grow antlers, and the antlers, while useful to defend against wolves, are most important for competing with other bucks to gain access to breeding does.

So long as adequate food is available, successive antler racks tend to get larger until a buck ages beyond his prime. A buck's antlers are formidable, and several people have been killed by "tame" bucks during the rutting season.

Many of the seasonal changes in deer biology and behavior are linked to environmental cues. The fall breeding season or rut actually begins during mid-August, when decreasing daylight triggers a hormonal chain reaction. Antler velvet begins to shed and necks swell. Sperm production peaks in mid-November, but continues through March.

The largest bucks become the main breeders. A dominant buck will breed most of the does in his home range, which he normally expands at this time of year. From December through February bucks drop their antlers.

Does come into estrus or heat during the rut and remain in estrus for about twenty-four hours. The does' increased urination frequency and nocturnal activity just before and during estrus improves communication and mating opportunities with the increasingly mobile and excited bucks. Estrus cycles may recur every twenty-five to thirty days from November through early March for does that have not become pregnant.

Gestation is 200 to 210 days, with fawns born primarily between mid-May and mid-June. Though not common, newborns have been observed as late as July. Single fetuses tend to be the rule for yearling deer; however, twins are more common in older does, and even triplets are possible. Does are in their prime from three to seven years old, but researcher Mike Nelson has seen does as old as seventeen years with a fawn.

Deer Feeding and Nutrition

Feeding, movement, and bedding make up the major daily activities of deer, with the most time invested in feeding. Generally, deer tend to be most active around dawn and dusk. In northern Minnesota's forests, weather probably has the broadest influence on deer activity. The historically severe winter of 1995–96 brought deep snow, cold temperatures, and windy conditions. Unusually large numbers of deer in north-central Minnesota then spent uncommonly long periods in shelter. The threat of wolf predation also interacts with weather to affect the deer's behavior.

Nutrition is critical to all other aspects of deer ecology. By mid- to late September, nursing fawns, having imposed the greatest energy drain of the year on their mothers, are weaned. As summer foods dwindle, deer graze more on grasses, sedges, and evergreen forbs. Large-leafed aster, bush honeysuckle, cherries, maples, bunchberry, and other species are still eaten when available. Deer in forested areas attain maximum weights and stores of fat in November.

Winter Adaptations

Winter is the most challenging season for northern

deer. During late autumn and early winter, the amount, availability, and quality of vegetation begin to diminish, and as winter progresses, deepening snow typically fosters a further decline in forage.

Northern deer have evolved an adaptive response. Most deer in northern Minnesota migrate in winter to protective conifer stands where they can save energy. Further, their highly insulated winter coat, a reduction in feeding, and decreased energy use for movement, enable deer to conserve energy.

An additional winter adaptation is a change in food. During late fall, deer begin eating largely woody browse that sticks up above the snow. Deer typically eat at least two dozen species in winter. As deer become more desperate during especially hard winters, they resort to lower quality pines, spruces, and balsam fir. Despite these adaptations, northern deer naturally lose weight during winter. I have seen deer so depleted of fat that if wolves had not killed them they would have died anyway.

As early as late March, increased daylight causes increased feeding, snow cover permitting, and increased metabolism. Energy costs also increase. As snow melts, movement becomes easier, and ground vegetation becomes increasingly exposed and available. Deer gradually supplement their browse diets with leaves, rejuvenated grasses, sedges, and forbs.

Prenatal Nutrition and Wolf Predation
Late winter–early spring coincides with the last third of pregnancy in northern does, which is when fetuses gain most of their weight. Gaining enough weight is critical to the fawn's viability at birth and its survival afterward. The body weights and fat reserves of does minimize by late May–early June, coinciding with their fawning period. Thus, it is not hard to understand why prolonged deep snow or late winter snowstorms can threaten not just the survival of the does, but that of their newborn fawns as well. With hungry wolves just waiting for a weakened deer, such problems can quickly prove fatal.

The nutritional recovery of deer as summer progresses into fall is critical not only to their survival the following winter, but it is also important to their fertility during the coming breeding season. Good nutrition at this time can lead to higher twinning rates, heavier fawns, and an increased ability of fawns to contend with mortality factors, especially wolves.

The Wolf and the Deer
Meanwhile, the wolves wait among the deer, seeking to exploit any weakness. If winter is harsh, the wolf's job is easier. If it is not, the wolf may have to search for a greater number of older deer or those with injuries. Nevertheless, over the long run, the populations of these two very different animals persist in spite of, and because of, the environmental vagaries described above.

Deer Movements, Populations, and Predation by Wolves
by Michael E. Nelson

As indicated earlier, winter weather largely influences the interactions between wolves and deer in Minnesota in a major way. The relationships among wolves, deer, and weather have been studied longest in northeastern Minnesota, where we have radio-tagged over 600 deer since 1973.

One of the main features of deer response to weather in northern Minnesota can be seen through their migration habits. Most northeastern Minnesota deer migrate up to fifty-five miles (88 km) each year between summer and winter ranges, which remain the same each year. The summer ranges of does in the area average about a third of a square mile (0.7 square km); bucks' ranges average one square mile (2.6 square km) or more. Their winter ranges are reduced by 50 to 90 percent.

While migrating, deer travel individually, with offspring, or female relatives for up to several days, depending on how far they have to go. Most migrations last less than four days. Essentially, all deer living in the northeastern Minnesota wilderness in summer leave during late fall or early winter (see chapter 7).

Deer Wintering Areas
There are four main deer wintering areas between Lake Vermilion and Lake Superior, and deer concentrate in them at 40 to 100 per square mile (104 to 259 per square km). Large numbers of deer wintering near Ely migrate in from a north-to-east arc. Deer wintering in the Mud Creek area west of Ely immigrate from a northwest-to-northeast arc. A smaller deer population winters at Isabella south of the Boundary Waters Canoe Area Wilderness (BWCAW), and they also migrate in from a northerly arc from west to east. Roughly 25 percent of them come from the BWCAW.

The fourth area lies along the north shore of Lake Superior. Deer near the Cascade River migrate inland toward the BWCAW during spring. We do not know, however, what percentage of north shore deer actually spend summer inside the BWCAW.

When deer were more abundant, many wintered throughout the wilderness as far to the northeast of Ely as Saganaga Lake. Milt Stenlund found numerous wolf-killed deer there from 1948 to 1952, as did Dave Mech from 1965 to 1973.

Snow depth below twelve inches (30 cm) and temperatures above freezing trigger spring migration, usually in March to mid-April. Fawns return with their mothers to the summer ranges where they were born.

About 20 percent of northeastern Minnesota deer fail to migrate to a summer range. They usually live year-round in heavily used winter ranges. Also, some deer winter at sites used by few other deer, and these deer usually also fail to migrate. Fawns generally copy their mother's migratory or non-migratory patterns, but migration behavior is learned, not innate.

Dispersal
Permanent movements away from birth sites constitute natal dispersal. Sixty-four percent of male fawns we radio-tagged in northeastern Minnesota dispersed from their natal home ranges as yearlings. Only 9 percent dispersed when two years old, and none when older. Unlike males, only 20 percent of females dispersed. Most yearlings dispersed less than 24 miles (39 km), but one female moved 105 miles (169 km) north, out of deer range and almost into caribou country.

Because most does do not disperse, those in any one locale are usually closely related. Many males disperse away from mothers and relatives, so they introduce new blood-lines. Biologists still disagree as to why deer disperse and why each sex does so differently.

An Evolutionary Arms Race
An evolutionary race between the deer and the wolf has shaped the traits of these animals. Deer slightly slower and less alert were killed first and eliminated from the gene pool that produced future deer. So, too, it was with wolves that were slower and less successful at catching deer. This process continues to this day.

Such evolutionary traits and their differences may move or be clustered depending on the pattern of male dispersal or female clustering. Each year's breeding season reshuffles the gene pool and produces individuals different in their ability to survive and reproduce. The differences, ever so slight, may be unimportant most of the time, but they may be critical when alertness, strength, and speed count. The characteristics we admire in deer today, such as the gracefulness of a deer's bound, result from a long evolutionary process of wolves killing deer, and deer escaping wolves. Thus, wolf predation plays a complex role that extends far beyond simply removing a deer from the population. Eventually the absence of wolf predation would result in deer somewhat different from those that evolved with wolves.

The spotted coat of newborn fawns blends perfectly with leaf litter and ground plants. Young fawns, unable to outrun wolves, instinctively hide during their first two weeks. Then, for a week or so, a disturbed fawn runs, then drops and hides. After that, fawns can outrun wolves most of the time.

Deer impress, frustrate, and stymie both humans and predators with their constant alertness which combines acute eyesight, smell, and hearing to detect strangers in their midst. Even while occupied, deer constantly twitch and rotate their ears, lift their heads, and strain the air currents.

The foremost of deer traits that impress us is their ability to jump from a standing position in a split second. Deer can clear an eight-foot-high (2-m-) obstacle, accelerate to thirty-five miles per hour (56 kph) with twenty-foot (6-m) bounds, and vanish in the blink of an eye. This behavior instantly puts distance as well as visual and physical obstacles between deer and wolves.

Deer and Wolves
From a circling aircraft in winter, I have seen deer remain alert as wolves walked within thirty feet (9 m) of them, only running if pursued, otherwise content to let the wolves pass. Several times I have watched as alert standing or bedded deer held their positions while wolves pursued other deer nearby.

Deer probably can identify terrain and vegetation that afford security. They often flee into water to escape wolves. During winter, I have observed deer standing on small bars in the middle of rivers while wolves lie along the shore. Wolves seem reluctant to charge into such situations, perhaps because their own footing and agility is compromised.

While water may mean security to deer, it does not always. One November, pilot Dick Mahl and I saw a deer swimming in Thomas Lake while seven wolves followed it from shore. After at least four hours of this, one wolf finally plunged into deep water from a fifteen-foot (5-m) cliff as the deer came close to shore. The wolf caught the deer by the neck, killed it, and towed it to its hungry packmates on shore.

Deer usually flee when approached by wolves. However, when their vigilance and fleetness fail, these prey animals can use their weapons. They rear up and flail at wolves with both forelegs. We once recovered a dead wolf with a fresh dent in its skull that nicely matched a deer hoof. Equally interesting were the wolf's four ribs well healed from previous breaks.

Deer also use their antlers against wolves. I once recovered a dead wolf with a lung punctured by an antler tip from the buck that the wolf's packmates eventually killed.

Deer belonging to groups seem to survive better than lone deer, as is true of most hoofed animals. More eyes and ears detect wolves sooner, and when wolves do attack, a large mass of moving bodies is more confusing to a wolf than is a single animal. In addition, in groups, risk is shared. Furthermore, groups of deer create trail systems that provide multiple escape routes. Where deep snow impedes escape, selection for grouping is intensified.

Not all deer escape wolves by running on packed trails. Some flee across frozen lakes. Often deer favor these lakes because of shallower snow and spend much time there.

In summer, deer do not need to group together. The firm ground and dense foliage, combined with a deer's quick acceleration and agility, allows for successful escape from wolf attack. Wolves killed less than 2 percent of our radio-collared deer in the snow-free months. Deer scatter on summer ranges, forcing wolves to search widely for vulnerable fawns. The more hidden and isolated a doe keeps her fawn, the less likely wolves will discover it. Although does re-form family groups later in summer, the fawns can escape wolves by this time. It is only with the coming of snow that smaller size again predisposes fawns to wolf predation.

Deer Population Dynamics
The number of deer in an area each year depends on how many died or dispersed and how many were born or immigrated in the previous year. Fawning brings a sudden increase, but deer numbers continually change as deer die throughout the year. A higher fraction of fawns die annually than of older deer. Typically, mortality peaks soon after birth and then again in winter.

Some 70 percent of fawns, 20 percent of adult does, and 53 percent of adult bucks we radioed died each year, on average, during a ten-year period of stable deer numbers in northeastern Minnesota. Similar proportions of each died in north-central Minnesota during part of the same period. A subsequent ten-year period of increasing deer was probably a result of lower fawn mortality due to fewer severe winters.

In northeastern Minnesota, wolf predation is the main mortality cause for fawns year-round and adults from November to April. Wolves killed roughly 20 percent of all adults, whereas hunters killed 30 percent of the bucks, the only sex hunted in the study area. In north-central Minnesota, wolves killed roughly 4 percent of each sex, and hunters killed 30 percent of the bucks and 15 percent of the does.

The only recent deer density data in wolf range indicate ten to twenty-six deer per square mile (per 3 square km) in north-central Minnesota and thirteen deer per square mile near Ely; six near Isabella; and one inside the BWCAW in 1986 and 1987.

Deer densities depend primarily on the severity of winters. The Isabella deer herd, for example, increased from 1985 to 1992 and stayed high, probably because starting in 1985, four consecutive winters were mild, and one was moderate, with average snow depths of only twenty-inches (51 cm) for only 60 days. During winter 1995–96, snow depths averaged over thirty inches (76 cm) for almost 120 days—the worst winter in twenty-seven years. Winter 1996–97 was similar, and deer declined.

It should be clear, then, that northern Minnesota deer numbers depend primarily on weather, with wolves, habitat, and human hunting having secondary influences, and all of these factors interacting. Many hunters believe that wolves reduce the number of deer they can shoot. Because of all these interactions, however, the situation is far more complex, as already discussed in chapter 7.

Minnesota Moose
by Patrick D. Karns

Although the primary prey of the wolf in Minnesota is the white-tailed deer, the current wolf range has historically held few if any whitetails. Instead, wolves fed mainly on two other members of the deer family, moose and woodland caribou (Figure 13). Both of these animals also played important roles in the native economy.

Caribou, however, were gradually overhunted, and none were left after 1929. White-tailed deer were rare in the area until well after the early twentieth century, when they out-populated moose. Moose declined from 3,000 in the early 1930s to 500 or fewer in the early 1950s.

During this era, many moose were reported dead and dying from a mysterious ailment known as "moose disease," which I, as a big game biologist in northern Minnesota, was to learn more about much later. Since 1960, however, moose have been increasing in northern Minnesota. A limited moose hunt has been allowed since 1971, and since 1989 the Indians of the 1854 Authority and Fond du Lac Bands of Lake Superior have also permitted hunting. Some 5,000 to 7,000 moose currently inhabit northern Minnesota.

Wolf Predation

Wolves prey heavily on newborn moose calves in June but continue to take some calves throughout their first year. When calves reach a year of age, however, and the new calf crop shows up, most of the yearlings are then safe from wolves and will be for several more years.

Moose calves are born in late May, weighing 25 to 30 pounds (11 to 14 kg) with reddish brown woolly coats that are exchanged for their first dark adult coats in late August. They grow rapidly, and by their first fall, when their growth stops for the winter, they weigh 350 to 400 pounds (159 to 182 kg). Growth resumes in spring. Cows reach their full weight of about 800 pounds (363 kg) in four to five years and bulls will weigh nearly 1,000 pounds (454 kg) in seven to nine years. Their massive weight and size are their main defenses against wolves.

Moose stand about seven feet (2 m) tall at the top of their hump. They can live to be twenty years old, although they start becoming especially vulnerable to wolves when nine to ten years old. Adult moose are dark brown to almost black with their lower legs an ivory yellow.

Most moose live their entire lives within a two-to-four-square-mile (5-to-10-square-km) area of where they were born. They have little need for the long nomadic movements of caribou that help thwart the wolves' attempts to find them, because moose are safe so long as they are strong and healthy.

Moose Reproduction

Bulls grow and shed their antlers each year; a set weighs 35 pounds (16 kg). Growth starts in April under the velvet, a fuzzy covering that provides the blood supply to the antlers while they are growing. The antlers reach their full size in late August, and the velvet dries. The bulls then polish their antlers by thrashing them on shrubs and trees.

Antler size determines the bulls' social status. Breeding cows have been known to leave one bull for another with larger antlers. Even though a moose never sees his antlers, he knows exactly how big they are and what his rank is. Bulls with smaller racks defer to him, bulls with equal antlers challenge, and bulls with larger racks are respected.

Fights are generally sparring matches with pushing and shoving until one animal gives up and leaves. The dominant bulls are the ones that generally breed the cows, who, when in heat, emit low moaning calls. The rut, or breeding season, covers the last week in September, and calves are born in late May after a 240-day gestation. Cows generally mature at twenty-eight months of age, and nearly all adult cows become pregnant, some with twins.

Heat Regulation

Form fits function in nature. Moose, being large and thus losing relatively less heat than smaller creatures, can thrive in some of the coldest climates, even with eight or more months of winter. Their large size and heavy winter coat of hollow hairs allow them to survive at forty degrees below zero and colder. Heat is a problem, so moose select habitats that allow them the most comfort. In their winter coat, they begin to show signs of heat stress at twenty-three degrees Fahrenheit (-5° C). The animals live in the north around the world.

In February, when daytime temperatures begin to rise and days become longer, moose head for shade under a canopy dominated by balsam fir and black spruce. In summer, temperatures above fifty-seven degrees Fahrenheit (14° C) are uncomfortable for moose, and they seek comfort in water or in damp shady stands of black spruce and balsam fir. It is quite a sight to see a moose almost submerged in some old swamp.

Food

Moose select their habitat to meet their seasonal needs for comfort and food; they need thirty to forty pounds (14 to 18 kg) of vegetation every day. During winter, moose eat 0.5 to 1.3 percent of their body weight daily and in summer, 2.6 to 3.5 percent based on dry matter. If the animals do not make their food quota, because of deep snow for example, they may well become food for wolves.

The year-round diet of moose in the mixed boreal forest of northeastern Minnesota includes twigs and leaves of willow, beaked hazel, red-osier dogwood, mountain ash, mountain maple, the sprouts of young aspen, paper birch, balsam fir, and dried aspen leaves. Moose sample almost any plant growing, but these are their mainstays. The word "moose" is Algonquin for "twig eater." In May and early June, moose frequent aquatic areas, aspen and birch, and upland stands of mature balsam.

Parasites

More so than many other animals, the moose itself is habitat for a number of interesting critters, either for their whole life or for some part of it. Most parasites harm their host little while others make the moose more susceptible to predators or accidents. A few kill the animal.

The winter tick is especially dangerous. Although the ticks' normal host is the deer, the winter tick is the only one that finds moose suitable, and most moose are probably infested with them every year. In some years, ticks may leave moose in poor condition or even kill them. The parasites can cause anemia and weight loss, and injure the coat so much that the moose dies of hypothermia in a spring storm. Of course, moose so weakened are ready prey for wolves. A single moose can harbor 50,000 or more ticks.

The most important of the six species of tapeworms that infect moose is the hydatid tapeworm, which lives in the lungs. This worm encysts as a larva and reproduces asexually; cysts can reach grapefruit size and contain thousands of larvae. Hydatid cysts in the lungs of moose can render moose vulnerable to wolves. When a wolf eats the cysts found in the moose's lungs, the larvae become tiny adults in the wolf's gut. The adults release eggs that pass with the wolf's feces and infect water and vegetation. When a moose swallows one of the eggs that has passed with the wolf's feces, it hatches, circulates to the moose's lungs, and encysts, completing the cycle.

Moose Sickness

"Moose sickness," has been reported since 1912. Afflicted moose lose their fear of man, walk in circles, and die. In the 1960s, sick moose fell under my jurisdiction. Not until Dr. Roy Anderson and his student Murray Lankester, Canadian biologists, learned that a parasitic worm caused moose disease did we realize what was behind it.

Dr. Keith Loken of the University of Minnesota and I found our first moose-disease worm in a wild moose at Bigfork, Minnesota. Then we checked brain specimens collected many years earlier and also found the same type of worm. Most people know it as the brain worm, but its scientific name is as formidable as the disease it causes—*Paraelaphostrongylus tenuis*.

P. tenuis normally inhabits white-tailed deer. It is the size of a hair and lives its adult life on the deer's brain, where it rarely causes problems. However, when it infects almost any other species of hoofed mammal, the worm penetrates the spinal cord and brain and causes numerous short circuits; similar to poking a fine wire into a computer.

Moose Mortality

Besides being prey for wolves and bears, moose are subject to all sorts of maladies and accidents. A few are killed by trains and cars every year. Arthritis is common in older moose, and many moose hold pus pockets where they have been jabbed by the antler tips of other moose. Occasionally we found a moose with antlers entangled in telephone lines. Moose would also drown after falling through thin ice, and poaching was probably a serious factor in keeping the moose population low prior to the 1960s.

Wolf predation on moose in Minnesota does not seem to reduce the population. The herd continues to grow at a healthy rate despite all of the accumulated mortality by bears, wolves, accidents, disease, and hunting by humans. While I worked in northeastern Minnesota, deer were numerous enough and so scattered throughout the country that wolves seldom preyed upon moose. No sick moose we investigated was ever bothered by wolves, and wolves never ate the carcasses we necropsied. Since then, however, virtually no deer have lived in the back country, at least during winter. Thus, moose are now very important in supporting the wolf population in much of the Boundary Waters Canoe Area Wilderness.

Suggested Reading

Fritts, S. H. and L. D. Mech. "Dynamics, movements, and feeding ecology of a newly protected wolf population in northwestern Minnesota." *Wildlife Monographs*, no. 80 (October 1981).

Fuller, T. K. "Population dynamics of wolves in north central Minnesota." *Wildlife Monographs*, no. 105 (1989).

Gese, E. M. and L. D. Mech. "Dispersal of wolves (*Canis lupus*) in northeastern Minnesota." *Canadian Journal of Zoology*. 69 (1969–1989): 2946–2955.

Harrington, F. H. and L. D. Mech. "Wolf howling and its role in territory maintenance." *Behaviour* 68 (1979): 207–249.

Mech, L. D. *The Wolf: The Ecology And Behavior of an Endangered Species*. Natural History Press. New York: Doubleday,1970; Minneapolis: Univ. of Minnesota Press, 1981.

Mech, L. D. and L. D. Frenzel, Jr. 1971. "Ecological studies of the timber wolf in northeastern Minnesota." USDA Forest Service Res. Pap. NC-52, St. Paul, Minn. 62 pp.

Mech, L. D. *The Way of the Wolf*. Stillwater, Minn.: Voyageur Press, 1991.

Nelson, M. E. and L. D. Mech. "Deer social organization and wolf depredation in northeastern Minnesota." *Wildlife Monographs*, no. 77 (July 1981).

Peters, R. and L. D. Mech. "Scent-marking in wolves: A field study." *American Scientist* 63, no. 6 (1975): 628–637.

Rothman, R. J. and L. D. Mech. "Scent-marking in lone wolves and newly formed pairs." *Animal Behavior* 27 (1979): 750–760.

Stenlund, M. H. *A field study of the timber wolf* (Canis lupus*) on the Superior National Forest, Minnesota*. St. Paul, Minn.: Minnesota Department of Conservation, 1955.

About the Contributors

Glenn D. DelGiudice received a B.S. degree from Cornell University (1977), a M.S. degree from University of Arizona (1982), and a Ph.D. degree from the University of Minnesota (1988). His research and publications include studies of the nutritional physiology and ecology of wolves, deer, elk, bison, and moose. Since 1990, he has been the deer project leader in the Forest Wildlife Populations and Research Group of the Minnesota Department of Natural Resources, and an adjunct associate professor at the University of Minnesota. Currently, he is conducting a long-term study of the effects of winter severity, nutrition, and diminishing conifer stands on white-tailed deer in north-central Minnesota.

Steven H. Fritts began studying wolves in Minnesota in 1972 and received a Ph.D. degree from the University of Minnesota in 1979 on wolves recolonizing northwestern Minnesota. From 1979 to 1984 he operated the U.S. Fish and Wildlife Service's (USFWS) wolf depredation control program in Minnesota. From 1984–89 he was section leader at the Endangered Species Research Branch of the USFWS, overseeing the Minnesota wolf research and other programs. In 1989 he became the wolf recovery coordinator for the northern Rocky Mountains, and then a chief scientist for the Yellowstone and Idaho wolf reintroduction program. Since 1996 he has managed USFWS research and endangered species grants for eight states. He has published forty-five articles on wolves.

Fred H. Harrington has a B.A. degree in biology from the University of Delaware (1965), and a Ph.D. degree from the State University of New York at Stony Brook (1975). His graduate research on wolf howling was conducted in northeastern Minnesota. After studying captive wolves and coyotes at Dalhousie University, Halifax, Nova Scotia, he was appointed to the faculty at Mount Saint Vincent University in Halifax, where he has since taught psychology and animal behavior. He has continued research on captive and free-ranging wolves through graduate students, published more than forty articles on wolves and other wildlife, and co-edited the book *Wolves of the World* (1982).

Patrick D. Karns, after completing his formal education at Michigan State University, joined the Minnesota Conservation Department in 1959, first as an assistant area game manager at Milaca, and in 1960 as the area wildlife manager for Cook, Lake, and St. Louis counties, headquartered in Ely, Minnesota. By 1965 he found himself frustrated by his lack of knowledge about the species he was managing, so he transferred to research. He spent the next twenty-five years as a part of a team helping to unlock the secrets of moose and white-tailed deer that would allow managers to know how these creatures contend with the annual cycle of seasons. Karns is enjoying his retirement in Wisconsin.

L. David Mech is a senior research scientist for the Biological Resources Division of the U.S. Geological Survey (formerly Division of Endangered Wildlife Research, U.S. Fish and Wildlife Service), and an adjunct professor at the University of Minnesota. With a B.S. degree in wildlife conservation from Cornell University in 1958 and a Ph.D. degree in wildlife ecology from Purdue University in 1962, he has studied wolves and their prey in several areas of the world for forty years and has published numerous books and articles about them. He has chaired the Wolf Specialist Group of the International Union for the Conservation of Nature and Natural Resources (IUCN) since 1978 and founded the International Wolf Center in Ely, Minnesota, (www.wolf.org) in 1985.

Michael E. Nelson is a wildlife biologist and field supervisor for the U.S. Geological Survey wolf research in northeastern Minnesota. Based at Kawishiwi Field Lab since 1974, he has studied deer and wolves for twenty-six years. During this time he completed his master's and Ph.D. degrees in wildlife conservation from the University of Minnesota. His research and publications examine deer movements, survival, population dynamics, social relationships, genetics, spatial ecology, and deer-wolf relationships.

Roger P. Peters graduated from the University of Chicago with a B.A. degree in political science, taught biology in West Africa as a Peace Corps Volunteer, taught mathematics at New College in Sarasota, Florida, for three years, and obtained his Ph.D. degree in psychology at the University of Michigan on scent-marking in wolves in northeastern Minnesota. He has published books on wolves, mammalian communication, and intelligence, and is a research associate at Lore International and the director of assessment at Fort Lewis College in Durango, Colorado.

Robert R. Ream is a wolf researcher and professor emeritus of wildlife biology at the University of Montana. He began working with wolves in the BWCAW with Dave Mech. In 1973, he started the Wolf Ecology Project at the University of Montana, which has studied natural recovery of wolves in Montana's Rocky Mountains. He was a member of the Northern Rocky Mountain Wolf Recovery Team and recently drafted a wolf management plan for the state of Montana. He served in the Montana House of Representatives for sixteen years and twice chaired its Fish and Game committee. He also serves on the board of the International Wolf Center.

Russell J. Rothman obtained a B.A. degree from Washington University in 1974. While there, he volunteered for the Wild Canid Survival and Research Center and assisted Richard Grossenheider in caring for twenty-five captive wolves, coyotes, and foxes. He earned his M.S. degree at the University of Minnesota in 1977 with Dave Mech, studying scent-marking and pair formation in lone wolves and newly formed pairs. For several years, he pursued his doctorate on wolves in Israel but then returned to the United States to begin a family and a business career. He continues his passion for conservation as co-chairman of the American branch of the Society for the Protection of Nature in Israel.

Editor's Note

Minnesota's wild wolves are wary and elusive. While wolf researchers get close to the animals using radio and capture collars, coming face to face with a non-collared, true wild wolf is a rare occurrence. Therefore, photographing wolves poses major challenges.

Almost all of the world's wolf photographs result from four approaches: opportunistic shots of wild wolves taken during wolf studies; close-ups of captive wolves in natural-looking surroundings; photos of wild wolves from afar; images of tame wolves temporarily released into the natural environment for the sake of photography.

To illustrate this book, it was necessary to select photos obtained by all these means.

The wolf is one of the world's most studied animals. Considerable information is available about the nature of the wolf: its social life, the composition of the pack in which it lives, its movements, reproduction, survival, and mortality. (Photograph © Alan & Sandy Carey)

Index

Page 128: (Photograph © Lynn M. Stone)